Art Therapy and PTSD

Richard D. Parsons, Ph.D.

cognella
SAN DIEGO

Bassim Hamadeh, CEO and Publisher
Amy Smith, Associate Editorial Manager
Casey Hands, Senior Production Editor
Jess Estrella, Senior Graphic Designer
Brianna Lucas, Licensing Associate
Natalie Piccotti, Director of Marketing
Kassie Graves, Vice President of Editorial
Alia Bales, Director, Project Editorial and Production

Printed in the United States of America.

To Greg Layton and so many others who are finding art to be a transformative space allowing that which is in … to come out.

Brief Contents

Detailed Contents

Cover Inscription

The art used for the cover of this text is the creation of Greg Layton, an artist, teacher, and social activist. Greg's work of over 3,000 paintings vividly chronicles his struggles, serving as a vital outlet for self-expression and a powerful pathway to healing. For Greg, as for so many others, art provides a transformative space to release what lies within, allowing that which is in … to come out.

Preface

Post-traumatic stress disorder (PTSD) is a pervasive and profoundly complex condition that affects individuals from all walks of life—veterans returning from combat, survivors of abuse and violence, first responders, and those who have endured personal loss or disaster. While traditional psychotherapeutic approaches such as cognitive behavioral therapy (CBT) and eye movement desensitization and reprocessing therapy have proven effective, there remains a growing recognition that such approaches are not viable for those clients who find discussing their traumatic experiences and memories to be too painful.

Art therapy offers a unique and powerful pathway for those struggling with PTSD, enabling them to externalize and process their experiences through creative expression. Art therapy provides a safe, nonverbal space for individuals to engage with their trauma on their terms, often revealing insights that words alone cannot capture.

While art therapy has traditionally been celebrated for its intuitive and subjective qualities, research is uncovering the neurobiological mechanisms that underpin its effects. For example, art-making has been shown to engage brain regions involved in emotional regulation and trauma processing, offering a direct pathway to address the physiological impact of PTSD.

This book, *Art Therapy and PTSD*, is designed to provide graduate students, clinicians, and researchers with a comprehensive understanding of how art therapy functions as a transformative tool for trauma recovery. Drawing from clinical case studies, neurobiological research, and trauma-informed therapeutic practices, it explores how art-making facilitates emotional regulation, self-reflection, and narrative reconstruction in trauma survivors, whether through drawing, painting, sculpture, or mixed media.

While each chapter is grounded in research, case illustrations and guided exercises help the reader move from understanding to application within their practice. This book aims to equip emerging art therapists and mental health professionals with the knowledge and skills to integrate creative art modalities into their trauma treatment.

Acknowledgments

I am fortunate to have the continuing encouragement, support, and competent assistance provided by all at Cognella Academic Publishing. I am particularly grateful for the expertise provided by Amy Smith, senior project editor; Casey Hands, production editor; and Kassie Graves, vice president of editorial, who remains an ever-present source of encouragement and energy.

Thank you, all.

PART I

An Introduction to PTSD and Art Therapy

CHAPTER 1

Post-Traumatic Stress Disorder (PTSD)

Trauma is an emotional response to a distressing or life-threatening event. It is possible that experiences such as war, violent crime, sexual assault, kidnapping, a fire, a car accident, or an attack by an animal can be sources of trauma. With trauma, an individual may experience difficulties sleeping, a general sense of nervousness, flashbacks of the event, and even unfeeling or numbness. The negative impact of trauma is experienced during and immediately after the traumatic encounter. With trauma, the distressing symptoms are most often not severe enough to interfere with daily functioning, and they gradually lessen and disappear over time. This is not the case for individuals with post-traumatic stress disorder (PTSD).

PTSD is a mental health diagnosis that applies when the symptoms of a traumatic experience persist and impair an individual's daily functions (Owens & Parsons, 2018). While the exact number of individuals experiencing PTSD is unknown, it has been estimated that PTSD affects approximately 6% of the U.S. population at some point in their lives (National Institutes of Health, 2024).

Trauma and PTSD represent significant challenges to an individual's psychological well-being and functional capacity. This chapter explores PTSD by examining its diagnostic criteria, symptomatology, neurobiological mechanisms, and approaches to treatment. Upon completion of the chapter, readers will be able to:

1. Describe the four clusters of symptoms presented by clients with PTSD;
2. Explain the role neurology plays in the experience of a client with PTSD, and;
3. Describe the traditional evidence-based psychotherapy approaches to the treatment of PTSD.

Diagnostic Criteria and Symptomatology

The experience of life-threatening or deeply distressing event(s) can result in an experience of trauma. While the impact of a traumatic experience is highly individualized, its impact can result in immediate and enduring consequences on an individual's emotions, cognitions, physiology, and behavior (Owens & Parsons, 2025) (see Case Illustration 1.1, note 1).

CASE ILLUSTRATION 1.1 This Cannot Be Happening[1]

The day started like so many days before. It was an overcast, wintry February morning, and Rachel started her routine morning walk with two dogs in tow. This "routine" soon became anything but routine or commonplace.

Rachel and her dogs stepped off the curb and crossed the alley each morning for the past three years as part of the final leg of their journey. However, all the previous experiences were without the sound of screeching wheels, a blaring horn, and the unexpected presence of a black hood of a car.

> *I can remember standing there in the middle of the crosswalk, seeing this car sliding right at me, and all I could think is that "this cannot be happening." I can't remember much from the incident except that everything seemed like it was in slow motion—my brain, my emotions, even my actions all seemed detached from me. I'm not sure how, but I released the dogs from my grasp and then found myself leaping up on the car's hood in my best action-movie hero fashion. All these actions seemed to be generated by someone else at another place and time.*
>
> *While my hood adventure helped me avoid being hit by the front of the car—the driver's sudden braking threw me 25 feet in the air. I stared at the cloud-covered sky, still thinking this could not be happening.*
>
> *As I lay on the ground, I felt numb, somewhat disconnected from the event and all around me. It was as if I was watching myself and the events unfolding, rather than experiencing them. All those gathered around me were talking but it just seemed like a Charlie Brown "wa-wa-wa"-type speech. Strangely, I was not upset or emotional (that came when they put me in the ambulance). I just remember being numb, detached, and continuing to think, this cannot be happening.*
>
> *Fortunately, the physical damage was minimal, but my dog-walking took a big hit. It was not that I was physically unable to do our morning walk; it was just that, for the first two weeks, I could not think about or speak about walking the dogs without "seeing" the hood of the car and feeling pretty much on edge.*
>
> *With the help and support of my spouse, I began to walk in the morning, eventually returning to the "scene." I still remember the incident, but now I experience it as a distant memory (now three months past) without any of the physical or emotional reactions that I first encountered following the incident.*

[1] The case illustrations throughout this book reflect actual clients. Unless otherwise specified, the details of the case and all identifying information have been changed to ensure client anonymity.

For some individuals, unlike Rachel (Case Illustration 1.1), the initial trauma is not adequately processed, and the trauma experience and consequences persist and progress to a point where the individual's functioning is significantly disrupted.

According to the American Psychiatric Association (2022), when symptoms persist for more than one month following a traumatic event and significantly impair functioning, then a diagnosis of PTSD can be assigned. PTSD is currently classified under Trauma- and Stressor-Related PTSD Disorders in the *Diagnostic and Statistical Manual of Mental Disorders* (2022). PTSD disrupts normal functioning in numerous domains.

Psychological and Cognitive Impact

The psychological consequences of trauma and PTSD are profound. Individuals often experience intrusive thoughts, nightmares, and flashbacks, which disrupt daily functioning and exacerbate feelings of fear and helplessness. Emotional dysregulation, including persistent anxiety, irritability, and depression, is common. PTSD can also impair cognitive functions such as memory, attention, problem-solving, and decision-making (Pitts et al., 2021). GEICO's classic Halloween "Good Choices: Horror Movie Commercial, 2014" (https://www.youtube.com/watch?v=Etx9h8AjDck0) presents an illustration of stress's impact on one's cognitive functioning. Given the choice of escaping an attacker by jumping into a running car versus entering a scary house and going to the basement, the car would seem to be the better choice. This, of course, requires rational thinking, which, as demonstrated in the commercial (hyping GEICO insurance as a good choice), has been put on hold given the stress the "victims" are experiencing.

Physical, Behavioral, and Emotional Consequences

Those struggling with trauma and PTSD often experience exaggerated startle responses, which can impair concentration and decision-making (Owens & Parsons, 2018). Chronic stress associated with PTSD can lead to heightened cortisol levels and increased vulnerability to cardiovascular, gastrointestinal, and immune-related disorders (American Psychological Association, 2024). Behavioral symptoms of hypervigilance and exaggerated startle responses reflect dysregulated autonomic nervous system activity.

While fear and a flight or fight response is expected when encountering significant stress or trauma, emotions and behavioral responses are typically short-lived, diminishing with the resolution of the event. However, for those with PTSD, emotional dysregulation—that is, the ability to control the intensity and valence (i.e., positive or negative) of one's emotional experience and expression—can be compromised (Conti et al., 2023).

Social and Interpersonal Effects

The social repercussions of trauma and PTSD can be devastating. Emotional dysregulation, characterized by irritability, anxiety, and depression, is common and can complicate interpersonal interactions (Bachem et al., 2021). Those with PTSD often withdraw from social engagements and experience difficulty trusting others, which makes it challenging to form intimate connections (Campbell & Renshaw, 2018). Marital discord, social isolation, and difficulty maintaining employment are common consequences of PTSD.

The experience of trauma is a foundational criterion for diagnosing PTSD. In addition, the diagnosis requires the presence of additional symptoms. Box 1.1 provides a summary of the four categories of symptoms experienced by those diagnosed with PTSD, and Case Illustration 1.2 demonstrates how a client may present these symptoms. Readers are referred to the American Psychiatric Association's *Diagnostic and Statistical Manual of Mental Disorders* (5th ed.; 2013; pp. 271–280) for a complete description of the diagnostic criteria.

BOX 1.1 PTSD Symptom Clusters

1. **Intrusion Symptoms**: Recurrent, involuntary, and distressing memories of the traumatic event; distressing dreams; dissociative reactions (e.g., flashbacks); intense psychological distress at exposure to cues; and marked physiological reactions to reminders of the trauma.
2. **Avoidance Symptoms**: Efforts to avoid distressing memories, thoughts, or feelings about the trauma and external reminders (e.g., people, places, activities) that elicit recollections of the trauma.
3. **Negative Alterations in Cognitions and Mood**: Inability to remember important aspects of the trauma, persistent negative beliefs about oneself or the world, distorted blame of self or others, persistent negative emotional states, diminished interest in activities, feelings of detachment, and inability to experience positive emotions.
4. **Alterations in Arousal and Reactivity**: Irritability or anger, reckless behavior, hypervigilance, exaggerated startle response, concentration difficulties, and sleep disturbances.

CASE ILLUSTRATION 1.2 Adrian: A 28-Year-Old Grocery Store Robbery Witness

The client, a 28-year-old male, is seeking therapy to address symptoms of post-traumatic stress disorder (PTSD) following a traumatic event. Six months ago, he was present during a violent robbery at a local convenience/grocery store. During the incident, guns were drawn and shot, mainly to get the store owner and this one customer's attention. The client, Adrian, witnessed the store owner being brutally beaten with a gun. The beating resulted in the owner's death. Throughout the experience, the client feared for his own life and still could not believe that he was left alive.

This experience has profoundly affected the client. In the first session with his therapist, he shared that he has been unable to function at work and generally wants to stay in his house. When asked to share what he has been experiencing, he noted:

- I cannot shake the memories and images of the event. Just walking past a store or hearing sudden loud noises throws me into panic (*intrusive symptoms; alteration in arousal and reactivity*);
- The thoughts and nightmares make it difficult for me to fall asleep or stay asleep (*intrusion symptoms);*
- I cannot concentrate at work, and I am constantly feeling pissed off (*alteration in arousal and reactivity*);
- I try to stay away from anything that reminds me of the robbery. I will not go to convenience stores or watch anything on television or in the news about robberies or crimes (*avoidances symptoms*);
- I cannot shake the feeling that I should have done something to help the store owner. I almost feel guilty for being alive (*negative alterations in cognition and mood*).

Neurobiological Underpinnings of PTSD

Advances in neuroscience have elucidated several neurobiological mechanisms underlying PTSD. Perry (2006), for example, reported the impact of trauma on the normal development of the brainstem (which regulates stress and metabolism), the midbrain (which plays a role in sleep and appetite), the limbic system (involved with regulating emotions and mood), and the cortex (which is associated with information processing and reasoning).

The experience of trauma can change the structure and functioning of the brain, particularly those circuits responsible for regulation of stress and emotions (Nemeroff, 2004).

It is believed that for those with PTSD, the trauma disrupted the normal functioning of the hypothalamic-pituitary-adrenal (HPA) axis, those areas of the brain that allow us to modulate our cognitive and behavioral responses to stress (Friedman & McEwen, 2004). It is also believed that the traumatic experience can disrupt the connectivity within fear-processing circuits, including the amygdala-prefrontal cortex-hippocampus network, thus exacerbating symptomatology (Kredlow et al., 2022).

Neuroimaging studies have identified heightened activation of the amygdala, the part of the brain critical for threat detection in those diagnosed with PTSD. This increased activity contributes to the individual's hypervigilance and exaggerated fear response (Sherin & Nemeroff, 2011). Compounding the problems is that for those experiencing PTSD, the part of the brain that modulates fear and stress responses, the prefrontal cortex, is often reduced in functioning, thus allowing for the exaggerated and unmodulated fear response (Henigsberg et al., 2019) (see Case Illustration 1.3).

CASE ILLUSTRATION 1.3 Adrian (continued): Exaggerated Fear Response

As the intake session continued, Adrian shared his feelings of being overwhelmed by his need to stay on guard. He noted that he cannot control his hypervigilance even though he is in a safe place at home or work. He finds that the most minor thing can cause an exaggerated fear response. He goes into full panic mode if there is a loud, sudden noise—anything coming close to sounding like gunfire. He described his most recent experience.

> *I am working on a contract when a car outside the office backfires. I actually peed my pants.*
>
> *My heart was pounding so hard that I was sure my co-workers could hear it. I felt like I was suffocating. I wanted to get up and run out of the office, but I was shaking so much I could barely stand. When I began to stand, I got very dizzy, and I thought I was going to pass out.*
>
> *My coworker Gail, who knows about my experience, came to my cubicle and helped me refocus and calm my breathing. Doctor, I cannot keep doing this.*

Evidence-Based Treatments

The evidence-based treatment of PTSD encompasses a diverse array of pharmacological, psychotherapeutic, and integrative approaches. Medications such as Sertraline, Paroxetine, Fluoxetine, and Venlafaxine (see American Psychological Association, 2017; VA/DoD Clinical Practice Guideline Working Group, 2017) have been employed in the treatment of PTSD. Research, however (e.g., Merz et al., 2019), shows that trauma-focused psychotherapies lead to more significant improvement in PTSD symptoms as compared to medications, and that these improvements last longer. Psychotherapeutic approaches empower individuals by enhancing self-efficacy, reducing feelings of helplessness and restoring control over one's life (Ehlers et al., 2005).

Psychotherapeutic interventions attempt to foster emotional processing by encouraging clients to confront and reappraise traumatic memories. When successful, this process diminishes the intensity of their fear responses and facilitates adaptive coping (Foa et al., 2007). Box 1.2 provides a brief description of some of the more traditional, evidence-based psychotherapeutic approaches to treating PTSD.

BOX 1.2 Evidence-based Treatment

Trauma-Focused Cognitive Behavioral Therapy (TF-CBT)

TF-CBT is a structured, short-term intervention that addresses trauma-related thoughts and behaviors. Key components include psychoeducation, relaxation techniques, cognitive restructuring, and exposure therapy. By targeting maladaptive beliefs and encouraging gradual exposure to trauma memories, TF-CBT fosters adaptive processing of traumatic experiences (Foa et al., 2007). A meta-analysis by Bisson et al. (2013) confirmed TF-CBT as a gold standard for PTSD treatment.

Prolonged Exposure Therapy (PE)

PE involves repeated and systematic exposure to trauma-related memories and stimuli. This process aims to extinguish the fear response and reduce avoidance behaviors (Foa et al., 2007). Studies have shown that PE leads to significant reductions in PTSD symptomatology, particularly in individuals with chronic PTSD (Powers et al., 2010).

Eye Movement Desensitization and Reprocessing (EMDR)

EMDR integrates elements of cognitive behavioral therapy with guided eye movements to facilitate adaptive processing of traumatic memories. The therapeutic mechanism involves accessing the traumatic memory network while engaging in bilateral stimulation, reducing the emotional intensity of the memory (Shapiro, 2007).

Cognitive Processing Therapy (CPT)

CPT focuses on modifying maladaptive cognitions related to the trauma. Patients learn to identify and challenge distorted beliefs, such as self-blame, while developing more balanced and realistic appraisals of the traumatic event (Resick et al., 2014).

Narrative Exposure Therapy (NET)

NET is a culturally sensitive intervention designed for individuals exposed to complex and cumulative trauma, such as refugees and survivors of war. By constructing a coherent narrative of their life and trauma experiences, individuals integrate fragmented memories and reduce symptoms of hyperarousal and avoidance (Schauer et al., 2011).

As is true for all areas of psychotherapy, no one approach works for every client. Standard treatments like those described in Box 1.2 are generally effective and are typically the treatments of choice. However, there are several challenges related to the most popular evidence-based therapies for PTSD. Patient engagement and satisfaction with these treatments can be problematic, especially for those clients for whom recalling and discussing their experience is retraumatizing. For these clients, there is often a high dropout rate and less than robust intervention responses (Lewis et al., 2020). With no-one-approach being universally effective, there is a need to refine existing treatments for PTSD and develop additional innovative approaches to provide more robust symptom relief (Maguen et al., 2023).

Innovative Interventions

Whether used as a standalone therapeutic approach or as a complement to more traditional modes of therapy, several innovative and integrative approaches have begun to expand the landscape of PTSD treatment. These appear to hold promise for treating clients with severe trauma, poor verbal memory and/or difficulties with talking about traumatic experiences.

Mindfulness-based stress reduction (MBSR) (Hopwood & Schutte, 2017) has effectively reduced avoidance behaviors and enhanced emotion regulations. MBSR has been reported as a valuable complement to traditional PTSD treatments (Boyd et al., 2018).

Yoga has also been shown to be associated with significant improvements in PTSD symptoms (see meta-analysis by Nejadghaderi et al., 2024). Yoga helps traumatized individuals tolerate physical and sensory experiences associated with fear and helplessness (van der Kolk et al., 2014).

Art therapy, which is the focus of this text, has been increasingly recognized as an effective treatment for individuals experiencing trauma and post-traumatic stress disorder (PTSD; e.g., Schouten et al., 2019). Clients engaged in art therapy can express through their visual work and through giving words to their artwork what it represents. This production can be reviewed and processed within the therapeutic relationship with the help of a therapist. A specific value of art therapy is that it provides a nonverbal, creative modality for processing trauma (Campbell et al., 2016; Malchiodi, 2022). This would be especially valuable for those clients who find it difficult to verbalize traumatic experiences.

The remaining chapters focus on the "what" and "how" of art therapy as a standalone and supplemental treatment for those experiencing PTSD.

From Knowledge to Application

As clinicians, whether in training or already in practice, expanding our understanding of the "what," "how," and "why" of art therapy as an effective treatment for those experiencing trauma and PTSD expands our tools and ability to be of service. However, knowledge and understanding are only a foundation for effective practice. Applying that knowledge is also necessary.

As such, each chapter within this book will end with a section entitled "From Knowledge to Application." Within this section, you will find an exercise that invites you to apply what you have learned by reading the chapter.

EXERCISE 1.1 The Profile of PTSD

Representation of characters with PTSD in movies can foster an understanding of and empathy for this condition. Several movies have depicted characters with PTSD in a realistic and relatable manner.

The following is a sampling of movies where the main character struggles with PTSD. Reviewing such a movie while attempting to identify the diagnostic symptoms can help move one from reading about to experiencing (while vicariously) PTSD.

Movie	Character	Description	What to look for ...
Taxi Driver (1976, Columbia Pictures)	Travis Bickle (Robert De Niro)	Vietnam War veteran who struggles with insomnia, isolation, and emotional detachment	Emotional viability and difficultly with interpersonal skills
Rambo (2008, Lionsgate Films)	John Rambo (Silvester Stallone)	A former Green Beret and Vietnam veteran	Anger, hypervigilance, and flashbacks
Silver Linings Playbook (2012, United International Pictures)	Pat Solitano (Bradley Cooper)	Trauma of catching his wife in an affair	Difficulty with emotional control and interpersonal relationships; also, a song as a trigger
Zero Dark Thirty (2012, Universal Pictures)	Maya Hansen (Jessica Chastain)	A CIA analyst, obsessed with finding Osama bin Laden, endures and witnesses multiple traumatic events throughout her pursuit	Emotional detachment, irritability, and a sense of constant threat

The Takeaway

Trauma is an emotional response to a distressing or life-threatening event, such as war, violent crime, sexual assault, or natural disasters. While trauma can cause temporary difficulties, such as disrupted sleep, flashbacks, and emotional numbness, these symptoms usually diminish over time. Post-traumatic stress disorder (PTSD), however, is a mental health condition that occurs when trauma symptoms persist and impair daily functioning (Owens & Parsons, 2018).

Effective treatment of PTSD requires a multifaceted approach rooted in evidence-based practices; innovative and integrative approaches like art therapy expand therapeutic options and appear especially useful for clients for whom verbalization about their experience is difficult.

Keystones

- Trauma is an emotional response to distressing or life-threatening events, such as war, violent crime, or natural disasters.

- Symptoms of trauma may include sleep disturbances, flashbacks, emotional numbness, and nervousness, which typically diminish over time.
- PTSD occurs when trauma symptoms persist for over a month and significantly impair daily functioning (Owens & Parsons, 2018).
- Approximately 6% of the U.S. population experiences PTSD at some point in their lives (National Institutes of Health, 2024).
- PTSD symptoms are grouped into four clusters:
  - Intrusive memories.
  - Avoidance behaviors.
  - Negative mood or cognitions.
  - Hyperarousal.
- The evidence-based treatment of PTSD encompasses a diverse array of psychotherapeutic, pharmacological, and integrative approaches. Meditation, yoga, and art therapy are emerging as innovative approaches to treating those with PTSD.

ADDITIONAL RESOURCES

Lopez Levers, L. (2022). *Trauma counseling: Theories and interventions for managing trauma, stress, crisis, and disaster* (2nd ed.). Springer.

Owens, E., & Parsons, R. D. (2025). *Crisis and trauma counseling: Unique forms of helping.* (2nd ed.) Cognella.

Parsons, R. D., & Owens, E. (2025). *Crises and trauma counseling: Professional and client self-help applications of evidence-based strategies.* Cognella.

REFERENCES

American Psychiatric Association. (2013). *Diagnostic and statistical manual of mental disorders* (5th ed.). American Psychiatric Association. https://doi.org/10.1176/appi.books.9780890425596

American Psychiatric Association. (2022). *Diagnostic and statistical manual of mental disorders* (5th ed., text rev.). American Psychiatric Association. https://doi.org/10.1176/appi.books.9780890425787

American Psychological Association (2017). *Clinical Practice Guideline for the Treatment of Posttraumatic Stress Disorder (PTSD) in Adults.*

American Psychological Association (2024). *Stress effects on the body.* American Psychological Association. https://www.apa.org/topics/stress/body

Bachem, R., Levin, Y., Zerach, G., Cloitre, M., & Solomon, Z. (2021). The interpersonal implications of PTSD and complex PTSD: The role of disturbances in self-organization. *Journal of Affective Disorders, 290,* 149–156. https://doi.org/10.1016/j.jad.2021.04.075

Bisson, J. I., Roberts, N. P., Andrew, M., Cooper, R., & Lewis, C. (2013). Psychological therapies for chronic post-traumatic stress disorder (PTSD) in adults. *The Cochrane database of systematic reviews, 2013*(12), CD003388. https://doi.org/10.1002/14651858.CD003388.pub4

Boyd, J. E., Lanius, R. A., & McKinnon, M. C. (2018). Mindfulness-based treatments for posttraumatic stress disorder: a review of the treatment literature and neurobiological evidence. *Journal of Psychiatry & Neuroscience, 43*(1), 7–25. https://doi.org/10.1503/jpn.170021

Campbell, M., Decker, K. P., Kruk, K., & Deaver, S. P. (2016). Art therapy and cognitive processing therapy for combat-related PTSD: A randomized controlled trial. *Art therapy: Journal of the American Art Therapy Association,* 33(4), 169–177. https://doi.org/10.1080/07421656.2016.1226643

Campbell, S. B., & Renshaw, K. D. (2018). Posttraumatic stress disorder and relationship functioning: A comprehensive review and organizational framework. *Clinical Psychology Review, 65*, 152–162. https://doi.org/10.1016/j.cpr.2018.08.003

Conti, L., Fantasia, S., Violi, M., Dell'Oste, V., Pedrinelli, V., & Carmassi, C. (2023). Emotional dysregulation and post-traumatic stress symptoms: Which interaction in adolescents and young adults? A systematic review. *Brain Sciences, 13*(12), 1730. https://doi.org/10.3390/brainsci13121730

Ehlers, A., Clark, D. M., Hackmann, A., McManus, F., & Fennell, M. (2005). Cognitive therapy for post-traumatic stress disorder: Development and evaluation. *Behaviour Research and Therapy, 43*(4), 413–431.

Foa, E. B., Hembree, E. A., & Rothbaum, B. O. (2007). *Prolonged exposure therapy for PTSD: Emotional processing of traumatic experiences: Therapist guide.* Oxford University Press. https://doi.org/10.1093/med:psych/9780195308501.001.0001

Friedman, M. J., & McEwen, B. S. (2004). Posttraumatic stress disorder, allostatic load, and medical illness. In P. P. Schnurr & B. L. Green (Eds.), *Trauma and health: Physical health consequences of exposure to extreme stress* (pp. 157–188). American Psychological Association.

Henigsberg, N., Kalember, P., Petrović, Z. K. & Šečić, A. (2019). Neuroimaging research in posttraumatic stress disorder—Focus on amygdala, hippocampus and prefrontal cortex. *Progress in Neuropsychopharmacology and Biological Psychiatry, 90* (2), 37–42. https://doi.org/10.1016/j.pnpbp.2018.11.003

Hopwood, T. L., & Schutte, N. S. (2017). A meta-analytic investigation of the impact of mindfulness-based interventions on post-traumatic stress. *Clinical Psychology Review, 57*, 12–20.

Kredlow, M. Alexandra, Fenster, R. J., Laurent, E. S., Ressler, K. J., & Phelps, E. A. (2022). Prefrontal cortex, amygdala, and threat processing: Implications for PTSD. *Neuropsychopharmacology, 47*(1), 247–259. https://doi.org/10.1038/s41386-021-01155-7.

Lewis, C., Roberts, N. P., Gibson, S., & Bisson, J. I. (2020). Dropout from psychological therapies for post-traumatic stress disorder (PTSD) in adults: Systematic review and meta-analysis. *European Journal of Psychotraumatology, 11*(1), 1709709. https://doi.org/10.1080/20008198.2019.1709709

Maguen, S., Madden, E., Holder, N., Li, Y., Seal, K. H., Neylan, T. C., Lujan, C., Patterson, O. V., DuVall, S. L., & Shiner, B. (2023). Effectiveness and comparative effectiveness of evidence-based psychotherapies for posttraumatic stress disorder in clinical practice. *Psychological Medicine, 53*(2), 419–428. https://doi.org/10.1017/S0033291721001628

Malchiodi, C. A. (2022). Frameworks for expressive arts therapy. In *Handbook of expressive arts therapy* (pp. 21–39). Guilford Press.

Merz, J., Schwarzer, G., & Gerger, H. (2019). Comparative efficacy and acceptability of pharmacological, psychotherapeutic, and combination treatments in adults with posttraumatic stress disorder: A network meta-analysis. *JAMA Psychiatry, 76*(9), 904–913. https://doi.org/10.1001/jamapsychiatry.2019.0951

National Institutes of Health (2024). *Post-traumatic stress disorder (PTSD) 2024.* https://www.nimh.nih.gov/health/topics/post-traumatic-stress-disorder-ptsd

Nejadghaderi, S. A., Mousavi, S. E., Fazlollahi, A., Motlagh Asghari, K., & Garfin, D. R. (2024). Efficacy of yoga for posttraumatic stress disorder: A systematic review and meta-analysis of randomized controlled trials. *Psychiatry Research, 340*, 1–14. https://doi.org/10.1016/j.psychres.2024.116098

Nemeroff, C. B. (2004). Neurobiological consequences of childhood trauma. *Journal of Clinical Psychiatry, 65*, 18–28.

Owens, E., & Parsons, R. (2018). *Crisis and trauma counseling: Unique forms of helping.* Cognella.

Owens, E., & Parsons, R. (2025). *Crisis and rauma counseling: Unique forms of helping* (2nd ed). Cognella.

Perry, B. D. (2006). Applying principles of neurodevelopment to clinical work with maltreated and traumatized children: The Neurosequential Model of Therapeutics. In N. B. Webb (Ed.), *Working with traumatized youth in child welfare* (pp. 27–52). Guilford Press.

Pitts, B. L., Eisenberg, M. L., Bailey, H. R., & Zacks, J. M. PTSD is associated with impaired event processing and memory for everyday events. *Cognitive Research: Principles and Implications, 7*, 35. https://doi.org/10.1186/s41235-022-00386-6

Powers, M. B., Halpern, J. M., Ferenschak, M. P., Gillihan, S. J., & Foa, E. B. (2010). A meta-analytic review of prolonged exposure for posttraumatic stress disorder. *Clinical Psychology Review, 30*(6), 635–641. https://doi.org/10.1016/j.cpr.2010.04.007

Resick P. A., Monson, C. M., & Chard K. M. (2014). *Cognitive processing therapy: Veteran/Military version.* Department of Veterans Affairs.

Schauer, M., Neuner, F., & Elbert, T. (2011). *Narrative exposure therapy: A short-term intervention for traumatic stress disorders after war, terror or torture* (2nd, expanded ed.). Hogrefe.

Schouten, K. A., van Hooren, S., Knipscheer, J. W., Kleber, R. J., & Hutschemaekers, G. J. M. (2019). Trauma-focused art therapy in the treatment of posttraumatic stress disorder: A pilot study. *Journal of Trauma & Dissociation, 20*(1), 114–130. https://doi.org/10.1080/15299732.2018.1502712

Shapiro, F. (2007). EMDR, adaptive information processing, and case conceptualization. *Journal of EMDR Practice and Research, 1*(2), 68–87.

Sherin, J. E., & Nemeroff, C. B. (2011). Post-traumatic stress disorder: The neurobiological impact of psychological trauma. *Dialogues in Clinical Neuroscience, 13*(3), 263–278.

VA/DoD Clinical Practice Guideline Working Group (2017). *VA/DoD clinical practice guideline for the management of posttraumatic stress disorder and acute stress disorder.* VA Office of Quality and Performance.

van der Kolk Laura, B. A., Stone, J., West, J., Rhodes, A., Emerson, D., Suvak, M., & Spinazzola, J. (2014). Yoga as an adjunctive treatment for posttraumatic stress disorder: A randomized controlled trial. *Journal of Clinical Psychiatry, 75*(6), 22573.

CHAPTER 2

Art Therapy

An Overview

Art therapy is a field of study and practice that merges the creative process of art-making with psychotherapeutic principles to foster self-expression, emotional healing, and psychological growth. This chapter explores the nature of art therapy, its theoretical underpinnings, and its application to the treatment of post-traumatic stress disorder (PTSD). Upon completion of the chapter, readers will be able to:

1. Describe the therapeutic impact of employing art therapy techniques when treating those experiencing emotional distress;
2. Describe the general focus and process of art therapy;
3. Explain the value of cultural sensitivity in art therapy.

The Emergence of Art as Therapy

The "therapeutic" value of artistic expression may be traced back to ancient cultures' use of cave paintings, totems, and symbolic drawings to promote communal and individual healing. However, a historical reference point for our discussion may be the works of Margaret Naumburg (1890–1983) and Edith Kramer (1916–2014). Both women are considered pivotal figures in the development of art therapy in the United States, each introducing distinct approaches that have significantly influenced the field.

Naumburg, an American psychologist and educator, is often called the "mother of art therapy." She founded the Walden School in New York City in 1915, emphasizing integrating creative arts into education (Naumburg, 1947). Drawing from Freudian psychoanalytic principles, Naumburg developed "dynamically oriented art therapy," which viewed spontaneous art expression as a pathway to accessing and articulating unconscious thoughts and emotions (Naumburg, 1966). She believed that art could serve as a form of symbolic speech, facilitating communication of internal conflicts that might be challenging to express verbally (Naumburg, 1947).

In contrast, Edith Kramer, an Austrian-born artist and educator, presented art as therapy. Kramer believed that the act of creating art was inherently healing. Unlike other approaches that used art primarily as a diagnostic tool or a means of communication, Kramer emphasized the therapeutic value of the creative process itself. Her focus was on the process more than the finished product. She felt that engagement in creative work could lead to psychological healing and ego development (Reinsbakken, 2017).

Like Naumburg, Kramer was influenced by psychoanalytic theory, particularly the concept of sublimation (i.e., the process of channeling unacceptable impulses into socially accepted actions). Kramer posited that the creative process could transform negative emotions into socially constructive outcomes (NeuroLaunch, 2024). She believed, for example, that a therapist working with art materials could assist a client for whom explosive aggression was an issue by allowing them to engage with materials such as clay. In this case, the tactile nature of the medium would allow the client to focus energy on the sensual manipulation of the clay, allowing for a positive outlet of the emotions (NeuroLaunch, 2024).

While Naumburg and Kramer recognized the therapeutic potential of art, their methodologies diverged. Naumburg utilized art to facilitate verbal psychotherapy, focusing on uncovering unconscious material through symbolic expression. One of her techniques involved the use of scribbling.

Naumburg (1947) would employ the scribble technique along with the client's verbal associations as a means of facilitating the client's sharing of difficult, personal material. The thought was that the use of scribble would allow the client to bypass normal resistances or defenses to tap those memories and experiences that have been relegated to the unconscious. Using large sheets of paper (e.g., 18″ × 24″), a size that would allow for expansiveness rather than constriction, clients would be provided drawing and coloring media and encouraged to draw a continuous and unpremeditated fluid line, stopping at whatever point they felt the scribble was complete (Hanes, 1995). The client would review the scribble, attempting to identify images formed by the intersecting lines, images that may reflect feelings or thoughts previously difficult to access.

Whereas Naumburg placed value on the product, and the verbal analysis that followed the creation, Kramer focused attention on the intrinsic healing properties of the creative process itself (Reinsbakken, 2017). Working at a children's residential treatment facility with boys exhibiting severe emotional and behavioral disorders, Kramer found that art could help redirect her student's negative emotions into art and self-expression. She believed that the process of finishing a piece of art was, in itself, healing (Genesis Inspiration Foundation, n.d.). Together their combined contributions have provided a comprehensive framework for art therapy, balancing the interpretive analysis of art products with an appreciation for the healing potential inherent in the creative process.

A Distinct Profession

While clinicians may employ art as a modality within their practices, art therapy is a unique and established mental health profession. It emerged with the establishment of organizations such as the American Art Therapy Association (AATA) in 1969. Academic programs and certification standards soon followed, contributing to the field's legitimacy and growth (AATA, 2023).

Art therapists must have a master's degree in art therapy or counseling or a related field with an emphasis in art therapy. They must complete the required core curriculum as outlined on the American Art Therapy Association's website (https://arttherapy.org/becoming-art-therapist/). Today, art therapy is practiced in diverse settings, including hospitals, schools, and community centers, and employed with clients experiencing difficulty with stress, anxiety depression, and trauma, the focus of this text.

Art Therapy Assisting Those with Emotional Distress

Art therapy helps individuals explore their emotions, gain personal insight, and develop coping skills. Art therapy utilizes the creative process to help individuals explore their feelings and emotions, gain personal insight, and develop coping skills (Malik, 2022).

Stress Reduction

Expressive writing, music, and art have been shown to positively affect psychological states and help reduce stress (Chanda & Levitin, 2013; Reynolds & Lim, 2007). Martin and associates (2018) reviewed 37 studies and found that participants had significantly reduced stress after engaging in one of four forms of arts interventions, including music therapy, drama therapy, dance/movement therapy, or art therapy.

When it comes to the act of creating art, it appears that such an activity engages an individual's parasympathetic nervous system (i.e., the quieting or resting system), reducing cortisol levels and, thus, promoting relaxation (Kaimal et al., 2016). These researchers (Kaimal et al., 2016) demonstrated that a 45-minute art-making session significantly lowered cortisol levels in 75% of the participants, irrespective of their artistic experience.

Anxiety

For individuals with anxiety disorders, art therapy has been shown to reduce symptoms by providing a calming and focused activity. The nonverbal AT approach holds value especially for clients who have difficulty in cognitive (re)labeling of their feelings or for whom talking about anxiety evokes fear (Smeijsters, 2008). The distancing from anxiety created by engaging with art improves cognitive regulation of emotions (Smeijsters, 2008).

Research (see Abbing et al., 2019; Schouten et al., 2015) revealed that art therapy significantly alleviates anxiety in clinical and nonclinical populations. For example, Abbing and colleagues (2019) reported on 47 women with anxiety disorders and found that 10 to 12 sessions of art therapy over 3 months reduced women's anxiety, improved their quality of life, and helped them regulate their emotions better.

Depression

Art therapy has also been found to be effective for individuals with depression. A study by Ciasca et al. (2018) revealed that participants with major depressive disorder experienced significant reductions in depressive symptoms after participating in group art therapy sessions. Bar-Sela et al. (2007) reported that patients undergoing chemotherapy experienced significant reductions in depression and fatigue levels after participating in art therapy sessions. Han and associates (2024), following a systematic review and meta-analysis, reported on the significant potential of visual art therapy (VAT) in ameliorating symptoms among individuals with depression.

Haeyen and associates (2024) found that engaging in art-making encourages individuals to explore different perspectives, engage in cognitive reframing, and find meaning in their experiences, which are valuable in treating depression. The creative process facilitated emotional exploration and fostered a sense of connection, which are critical in managing depression (see Case Illustration 2.1).

Trauma

Traditional therapeutic approaches, such as cognitive-behavioral therapy (CBT), pharmacotherapy, and eye movement desensitization and reprocessing (EMDR), have proven effective in assisting those who experience trauma and emotional distress (APA, 2025). However, it has been reported that over one-third of clients do not benefit from these interventions (Bradley et al., 2005). This appears particularly true for clients with severe trauma, a poor verbal memory, and/or difficulties with talking about traumatic experiences.

CASE ILLUSTRATION 2.1 Damn, I Miss Her

Jerome, a 49-year-old steel worker, came to therapy at his sister's request. His sister expressed concern that Jerome has been socially withdrawn, drinking more than usual, and appearing depressed. According to her, this all began five weeks ago after the death of their 84-year-old mother. According to Jerome's sister, she was concerned that Jerome was not addressing his grief or depression. She asked him to go to therapy as a favor to her.

During the initial session, Jerome avoided any discussion of his mother's death. When asked how he felt about all that had happened, he attempted to minimize it by saying, "Hey, she was old—had a good life—we all have to go one day."

After explaining the nature of art therapy and the goals that the process may achieve, the therapist invited Jerome to work with clay. Initially, while less than enthusiastic about the process, he complied. The therapist invited him to close his eyes and manipulate the clay in any way he wished. The goal was to get him to elevate the sensory experience of touching the clay. When asked about the experience, Jerome noted that it felt somewhat relaxing. He was then asked to keep his eyes closed and craft something to remind him of his mother.

The process, being ill-defined and highly sensorial, triggered the expression of several emotions, starting with frustration and annoyance at the therapist. "How am I supposed to make something? I am not a sculptor and cannot see what I am doing." As he continued with the clay, his anger turned to anxiety and sadness. "I'm not sure how to do this; I might screw it up. I screw up everything."

The therapist provided assurance and directed him to focus on the clay, feel it, and allow his hands to do whatever he felt. With the therapist's direction and support, Jerome began to roll the clay into a cylindrical shape. As he molded the clay, he began to cry. After a few minutes, he stopped, opened his eyes, and shared, "Every Sunday, when I was a kid, my mom and I would make cinnamon rounds. My job was to roll the dough into hot-dog-shaped tubes, which she would cut for baking. She used to say I was her best helper." With this last statement, Jerome, now tearful, opened his eyes. "Her best helper? I could not even help her when she needed it most. Damn, I miss her so much."

The pain of the loss that he now experienced and expressed became the focus of subsequent sessions.

Alternative interventions like art therapy are gaining traction due to their holistic and creative focus. Creative activities, such as painting, clay modeling, or collage, can assist clients in accessing and expressing emotions that may be difficult to verbalize or recognize. Artistic materials can help clients access and process memories safely and step-by-step (Spiegel et al., 2006). As will be presented throughout the remainder of this text, art therapy is a creative and effective approach to treating PTSD.

Focus Points and Processes

Therapy cannot be employed as a fixed formula or template in any form or modality. It takes shape in response to each client's uniqueness, goals and challenges, and the nature of the therapeutic relationship. With that caveat, art therapists working with clients who experience PTSD employ several focus points or targets.

Creating a Therapeutic Alliance

Art therapy, as is proper for all psychotherapy, works within the context of a therapeutic relationship and alliance. With art therapy, the actual art product is a prime constituent of therapeutic interventions. It can add a third dimension to the therapeutic alliance to form a triangular relationship between the art therapist, the client, and the artwork (Schaverien, 2000). Art therapist, as is true of all therapist, attempt to create a therapist-client relationship in which the client feels safe, feels free to express themselves without judgment, and is understood. In addition, and unique to art therapy, they are also conscious of the nature of the materials and the task employed since these contribute to the creation of a working alliance (Gazit et al., 2021). This is particularly vital when working with those with PTSD and who may feel particularly vulnerable.

Goal Setting

Art therapists gather data on the client's history, symptoms, and therapeutic goals during the initial session. They may use standardized tools, interviews, and initial art exercises to gauge the client's emotional state and artistic comfort level (Malchiodi, 2020).

One unique strategy employed in art therapy for the goal identification is road drawing (Hanes, 1995). When creating a road drawing, a client is asked to "draw a road" using drawing materials, such as colored pencils, markers, oil pastels, chalk pastels, or graphite pencils. Clients may be invited to consider various aspects of a road, such as its windy nature, the presence of potholes, the location, and most certainly the destination. In drawing a road, clients can explore where they have been, where they are, and where they wish to go.

Selecting Art Form and Mediums

The use of diverse mediums—such as painting, drawing, or sculpting—allows clients to choose forms of expression that resonate with them. In most cases, the client selects the medium and form, thus promoting agency and control over their healing process. It is not unusual, however, for the therapist to offer suggestions and guidance so that the medium and the "project" align with the therapeutic goals (see Case Illustration 2.2).

CASE ILLUSTRATION 2.2 Self-Empowerment

Client Background: Rosalie, a 35-year-old lawyer, came to therapy following her recent divorce. Rosalie shared that the divorce, which came at the initiation of her husband of five years, was a total shock and surprise. "I did not see it coming. I feel like a total fool, completely out of touch with reality. How could I not see he was unhappy?" As she continued, she noted that she focused on building her career. "All my time—energy—and focus was on building my firm, and you know what, that's even failing. I feel like everything is out of control."

Several goals were established, including fostering a sense of self-empowerment, agency, and control. This goal directed Dr. Harboe to use art materials in the session.

Medium Selection in Art Therapy

Rosalie was introduced to various art materials, including drawing pencils, pastels, acrylic paints, clay, charcoal, and collage materials and invited to select what she might want to use. However, she had difficulty selecting.

Dr. Harboe reminded Rosalie that one of her goals was to gain some control and sense of agency over the symptoms she was experiencing. With that as a focus, Rosalie selected charcoal, stating, "I feel like I can erase and start over easily if I screw up." This choice reflected her need for control in the creative process.

As her first exercise, Rosalie was invited to create an image representing her current internal experience. She used charcoal to draw a dark scene with jagged lightning and swirling winds, covering the entire page with charcoal.

Looking at her finished product, she stated, "I hate this—it is dirty and chaotic." She smudged the drawing, smoothing edges and removing charcoal to open a white background. When invited to share her experience, she noted:

> It's hard to explain. Having the ability to smudge the drawing, making it less ominous and less chaotic, felt cathartic. When I started smudging the drawing, I felt angry. I felt it was controlling me, not me creating it. I wanted to destroy it. But as I felt the charcoal and my hands glide across the paper and began seeing that the drawing could be changed, I relaxed and felt more in control. I realized that I could choose what stays and what goes. I guess that's true for my life as well.

This case highlights the importance of honoring client preferences for specific art materials. Rosalie's choice of charcoal provided an accessible and safe medium for emotional exploration, aligning with her therapeutic goals of gaining control, agency, and self-empowerment.

Connecting Experience and Expression

Themes and issues targeted in art therapy include emotion regulation, resilience, a sense of control and agency, and the narrating and processing traumatic experiences (Kaimal et al., 2020). Throughout the creative process, the therapist assists the client in connecting their sensory experiences of trauma to their artistic expression, helping them facilitate a deeper understanding and reprocessing. The integration of sensory memories with declarative memory, which is facilitated through the process of art therapy, has been shown to reduce symptoms of PTSD (Campbell et al., 2016).

Session Markers

While each session and experience reflect the uniqueness of the client and the nature of the therapeutic relationship, the session will often hit specific markers guiding the process. Starting with a *check-in* to assess the client's current concerns, emotional state, and recent experience, the therapist and client would highlight the goals being addressed. They would then engage the client with the chosen art form (e.g., drawing, painting, sculpting). During this time and process, the therapist and client, working collaboratively, will explore connections to emotions that may have surfaced, memories or images that may have emerged, and the client's personal experience with the process. Should the client experience difficult emotions, the therapist may use additional strategies, such as relaxation methods, cognitive reframing, or grounding exercises, to help the client work through these emotions.

The final stage of a session typically involves integrating insights gained through the experience into daily life and fostering coping strategies. Therapists may encourage clients to maintain an art journal or engage in independent creative activities as a form of self-care (Malchiodi, 2020).

Cultural Considerations in Art Therapy

Cultural considerations must be central to art therapy, as they are to all therapeutic encounters. Art is both a universal language and a culturally specific medium. Art therapists must navigate cultural variations in symbols, meanings, and communication styles to foster an inclusive therapeutic environment.

A constructivist approach to art therapy emphasizes the contextual nature of meaning-making, emphasizing that cultural background shapes how individuals interpret their artwork and therapeutic experiences (Kapitan, 2010). Understanding the cultural context of a client's artwork is essential for accurate interpretation and meaningful dialogue. The American Art Therapy Association (2011) emphasizes the need for art therapists to be culturally competent.

> Culturally competent art therapists are able to design and offer art therapy interventions and experiences that take into consideration their clients' diverse art traditions, preferences for art materials, and their beliefs and practices related to the creation of imagery. (2011, III, C.2)

Incorporating culturally relevant art forms, symbols, and themes and using culturally familiar materials (traditional textiles, indigenous art supplies) can create a sense of comfort and connection and enhance the therapeutic alliance and treatment outcomes. However, art therapists must be sensitive to such nuances since artwork's symbols, colors, and themes often carry distinct meanings within specific cultural contexts.

For example, colors carry profound emotional and symbolic meanings that vary widely across cultures. Art therapists must recognize that color choices in clients' artworks are not arbitrary; cultural narratives and personal experiences inform them. Not considering these cultural connotations can lead to misinterpretation (see Case Illustration 2.3).

CASE ILLUSTRATION 2.3 Not Peace—Grief

Client Background: Aisha, a 47-year-old university art teacher, immigrated with her family from China when she was 18. Aisha came to therapy following the death of her father. She reported feelings of deep sadness and emotional numbness. However, she was frustrated because she had been unable to show her emotions or even find the words to express the depth of her grief adequately.

A Misinterpretation

In her second art therapy session, Aisha was invited to create an artwork that expressed her emotions. She chose to work primarily with white paint, creating an abstract work of a spiraling cone, which became brighter and whiter near its apex. The art therapists, unfamiliar with the cultural significance of white in Chinese mourning traditions, interpreted Aisha's choice and presentation as reflecting her progress and movement toward peace and serenity.

While being polite, Aisha was both confused and somewhat irritated by the therapist's interpretation. "Forgive me. You keep talking about peace, but that is not how I feel. The white is not peaceful—it is heavy. It is my mourning, and it is increasing, not diminishing."

It was clear that the therapist's projection of a Western association with white (purity and serenity) in Aisha's artwork created a sense of disconnection and invalidation of her emotional experience. Recognizing the mistake, the therapist apologized and acknowledged his cultural blind spot. He invited Aisha to share more about the significance of white in her culture and how it related to her grieving process. This opened a meaningful dialogue, allowing Aisha to explain how white symbolized the sacredness and depth of her mourning.

From Knowledge to Application

Art therapy distinguishes itself from other forms of psychotherapy by integrating the creative process of making art with therapeutic techniques to foster emotional, psychological, and social well-being. The act of making art is inherently therapeutic. Engaging in creative activities can stimulate flow, reduce stress, and promote relaxation. Exercise 2.1 invites you to experience the value of engaging in such creative activities.

EXERCISE 2.1 Two Mediums

Directions: This exercise invites you to be your art therapy client. Identify a recent event or scenario in which you had a substantial adverse emotional reaction (e.g., anger, shame, guilt, anxiety ... sadness). Take a moment to remember as many details as possible and how you felt at the time.

Part 1: Drawing

Using paper and some varied colored writing implements (pencils, crayons, paints), draw something or make a visual design that represents the emotions you experienced then and may have re-experienced as you just now reflected on the incident.

Part 2: Clay-work

Gather some clay; if none is available, make "clay" with one cup of flour and one cup of salt. Slowly add up to one-half cup of cold water while mixing to form a ball. It helps to knead the clay for several minutes. Once you have your clay:

a. Close your eyes and try to remember the upsetting scenario and how you felt. Try to hold those thoughts and feelings as you squeeze and manipulate the clay with your hands. Allow your focus to shift from the event and your feelings at a time to the sensory experience of working with the clay. Take time to become aware of your body sensations and emotional experiences while engaging with the clay.

b. Open your eyes. Use your clay to create something that gives form to your feelings about that event.

Reflecting on the experiences

Drawing

1. How would you describe your experience of using colored pens to create a representation of the negative feelings you had identified?
2. Remembering how you felt when you began to remember the incident, did working with the art impact those feelings?
3. What value or benefit do you feel engaging with this art medium and project had for you?

Clay

1. How would you describe your experience manipulating clay in your hands?
2. How would you describe your experience using clay to represent the negative feelings you identified and may have re-experienced at the beginning of this exercise?
3. Remembering how you felt when you began to remember the incident, did manipulating the clay and/or using it in creating a project impact these feelings?
4. What value or benefit do you feel engaging with this art medium and project had for you?

The Takeaway

Art therapy, rooted in the inherent therapeutic value of artistic expression, has evolved from ancient cultural practices to a structured discipline with significant contributions from pioneers like Margaret Naumburg and Edith Kramer. The field of art therapy gained professional recognition with the establishment of the American Art Therapy Association (AATA) in 1969, which standardized academic programs and certification processes. Today, art therapy addresses a wide range of psychological and social challenges, utilizing creative processes to promote healing, self-expression, and reconsolidation of traumatic memories. Its integration of cultural sensitivity ensures its adaptability across diverse populations and settings.

Keystones

- Art as a form of psychotherapy can be traced back to Margaret Naumburg's "dynamically oriented art therapy" and Edith Kramer's emphasis on the creative process's healing power.
- Art therapy is practiced in diverse settings, including hospitals, schools, and community centers. It is employed with clients with varying issues, from trauma and mental illness to developmental challenges and end-of-life care.
- Art therapy facilitates the nonverbal expression of emotions and traumatic memories.
- Art therapy promotes psychological healing through creativity, self-expression, and reconsolidation of trauma.

- Art therapists must recognize the importance of culturally relevant symbols, colors, and themes and engage clients with cultural sensitivity.

ADDITIONAL RESOURCES

Case, C., Dalley, T., & Reddick, D. (2023). *The handbook of art therapy* (4th ed.). Routledge.

Henley, D. R. (2024). *The Kramer method of art therapy: Exploring the third hand.* Charles C. Thomas.

Rastogi, M., Feldwisch, R.P., Pate, M., & Scarce, J. (Eds.) (2022). *Foundations of art therapy: Theory and applications.* Academic Press.

Van Lith, T., & Ettenberger, M. (2023). Arts-based therapies, practices, and interventions in health. *BMC Complementary Medicine and Therapies* 23, 351. https://doi.org/10.1186/s12906-023-04177-4

REFERENCES

Abbing, A., de Sonneville, L., Baars, E., Bourne, D., & Swaab, H. (2019). Anxiety reduction through art therapy in women: Exploring stress regulation and executive functioning as underlying neurocognitive mechanisms. *PloS One, 14*(12), e0225200. https://doi.org/10.1371/journal.pone.0225200

American Art Therapy Association. (2011). *Art therapy multicultural/diversity competencies.* American Art Therapy Association. https://arttherapy.org/wp-content/uploads/2017/06/Multicultural-Competencies.pdf

American Art Therapy Association. (2023). *About art therapy.* American Art Therapy Association. https://arttherapy.org/becoming-art-therapist/

American Psychological Association. (2025). *Clinical practice guideline for the treatment of posttraumatic stress disorder (PTSD) in adults.* American Psychological Association. https://www.apa.org/ptsd-guideline/ptsd.pdf

Bar-Sela, G., Atid, L., Danos, S., Gabay, N., & Epelbaum, R. (2007). Art therapy improved depression and influenced fatigue levels in cancer patients on chemotherapy. *Psycho-oncology, 16*(11), 980–984. https://doi.org/10.1002/pon.1175

Bradley, R., Greene, J., Russ, E., Dutra, L., & Westen, D. (2005). A multidimensional meta-analysis of psychotherapy for PTSD. *American Journal of Psychiatry, 162*(2), 214–227.

Campbell, M., Decker, K. P., Kruk, K., & Deaver, S. P. (2016). Art therapy and cognitive processing therapy for combat-related PTSD: A randomized controlled trial. *Art Therapy: Journal of the American Art Therapy Association, 33*(4), 169–177. https://doi.org/10.1080/07421656.2016.1226643

Chanda, M. L., & Levitin, D. J. (2013). The neurochemistry of music. *Trends in Cognitive Sciences, 17*(4), 179–193.

Ciasca, E. C., Ferreira, R. C., Santana, C. L. A., Forlenza, O. V., Dos Santos, G. D., Brum, P. S., & Nunes, P. V. (2018). Art therapy as an adjuvant treatment for depression in elderly women: A randomized controlled trial. *Brazilian Journal of Psychiatry, 40*(3), 256–263.

Gazit, I., Snir, S., Regev, D., & Bat Or, M. (2021). Relationships between the therapeutic alliance and reactions to artistic experience with art materials in an art therapy simulation. *Frontiers in Psychology, 12*, 560957. https://doi.org/10.3389/fpsyg.2021.560957

Genesis Inspiration Foundation (n.d.). *Edith Kramer: The mother of art therapy.* Genesis Inspiration Foundation. https://genesisinspirationfoundation.org/the-mother-of-art-therapy/

Han, B., Jia, Y., Hu, G., Bai, L., Gains, H., You, S., Rendon, H., R., Jiao, Y. Huang, K., Cui, L. & Chen, L. (2024). The effects of visual art therapy on adults with depressive symptoms: A systematic review and meta-analysis. *International Journal of Mental Health Nursing, 33*(5), 1183–1196.

Hanes, M. J. (1995). Clinical application of the "scribble technique" with adults in an acute inpatient psychiatric hospital. *Art Therapy, 12*(2), 111–117.

Kapitan, L. (2010). *An introduction to art therapy research.* Routledge., G., Jones, J. P., Dieterich-Hartwell, R., & Wang, X. (2020). Long-term art therapy clinical interventions with military service members with traumatic brain injury and post-traumatic stress: Findings from a mixed methods program evaluation study. *Military Psychology: The Official Journal of the Division of Military Psychology, American Psychological Association, 33*(1), 29–40. https://doi.org/10.1080/08995605.2020.1842639

Kaimal, G., Ray, K., & Muniz, J. (2016). Reduction of cortisol levels and participants' responses following art making. *Art Therapy: Journal of the American Art Therapy Association, 33*(2), 74–80. https://doi.org/10.1080/07421656.2016.1166832

Kapitan, L. (2010). *An introduction to art therapy research.* Routledge.

Malchiodi, C. A. (2020). *Trauma and expressive arts therapy: Brain, body, and imagination in the healing process.* Guilford Press.

Malik, S. (2022). Using neuroscience to explore creative media in art therapy: A systematic narrative review. *International Journal of Art Therapy, 27*(2), 48–60.

Martin, L., Oepen, R., Bauer, K., Nottensteiner, A., Mergheim, K., Gruber, H., & Koch, S. C. (2018). Creative arts interventions for stress management and prevention—a systematic review. *Behavioral Sciences, 8*(2), 28. https://doi.org/10.3390/bs8020028

Naumburg, M. (1947). *Studies of the "free" art expression of behavior problem children and adolescents as a means of diagnosis and therapy.* Coolidge Foundation.

Naumburg, M. (1966). *Dynamically oriented art therapy: Its principles and practices, illustrated with three case studies.* Grune & Stratton.

NeuroLaunch (2024). *Edith Kramer: Pioneering art therapy and transforming lives through creativity.* NeuroLaunch. https://neurolaunch.com/edith-kramer-art-therapy/

Reinsbakken, M. (2017). *The grandmothers.* ArtBeat Art Therapy Studio. https://www.artbeatarttherapystudio.com/the-history-of-art-therapy-in-canada-too-eh/march-01st-2017

Reynolds, F., & Lim, K. H. (2007). Contribution of visual art-making to the subjective well-being of women living with cancer: A qualitative study. *The Arts in Psychotherapy, 34*(1), 1–10.

Schaverien, J. (2000). The triangular relationship and the aesthetic countertransference in analytical art psychotherapy. In A. Gilroy & G. McNeilly (Eds.), *The changing shape of art therapy: New developments in theory and practice* (pp. 55–83). Jessica Kingsley Publishers.

Schouten, K. A., de Niet, G. J., Knipscheer, J. W., Kleber, R. J., & Hutschemaekers, G. J. M. (2015). The effectiveness of art therapy in the treatment of traumatized adults: A systematic review on art therapy and trauma. *Trauma, Violence & Abuse, 16*(2), 220–228.

Smeijsters, H. (2008). *Handboek creatieve therapie.* Coutinho.

Spiegel, D., Malchiodi, C., Backos, A., & Collie, K. (2006). Art therapy for combat-related PTSD: Recommendations for research and practice. *Art Therapy, 23*(4), 157–164.

CHAPTER 3

The Role of Creativity in Trauma Recovery

Psychological interventions such as trauma-informed cognitive behavior therapy (CBT), cognitive processing therapy, and exposure therapies remain a mainstay in the treatment of trauma and post-traumatic stress disorders (APA, 2025). However, engagement in creativity, specifically *art therapy*, is increasingly recognized as an effective intervention for individuals experiencing trauma and post-traumatic stress disorder (PTSD), especially those with poor verbal memory or difficulties in discussing traumatic experiences (Heijman et al., 2024).

Art therapy integrates principles from psychology, neuroscience, and the creative arts to promote healing and self-expression (Malchiodi, 2020). The visual, tangible, and experiential nature of visual art therapy reflects the visual, sensory, and wordless nature of a traumatic experience and memories (Malchiodi, 2020). Additionally, art therapy, emphasizing creativity and self-expression, fosters engagement and intrinsic motivation, enhancing treatment adherence (Haeyen & Wanten, 2024).

This chapter explores three key dimensions of creativity and art therapy in trauma recovery: (1) the neurological impact of creative processes, (2) the facilitation of the retrieval and reconsolidation of traumatic memories, and (3) the re-establishment of emotional regulation. Upon completion of the chapter, readers will be able to:

1. Describe the impact of trauma on the brain's neuroplasticity and ability to engage in emotional regulation;
2. Explain how creativity and art therapy facilitate the retrieval and reconsolidation of traumatic memories, and;
3. Explain the process by which art therapy supports clients with PTSD in their review, reframing, and verbal discussion of their traumatic experience.

Neurological Impact of Art Therapy

As noted in Chapter 1, trauma can affect brain function and structure. Advances in cognitive neuroscience, especially neuroimaging, have provided insight into the neurological mechanisms that make art therapy a potent tool for mental health intervention. Symptoms of PTSD have been connected to stress-induced changes in brain structure and function. Brain regions that are felt to play an important role in PTSD include the hippocampus (memory), the amygdala (emotional arousal), and the medial prefrontal cortex, which serves to modulate emotional responsiveness through inhibition of amygdala function (Bremner, 2007). Additionally, it is now believed that trauma impacts the normative functioning of the Default Mode Network (DMN) (Brandman et al., 2021).

Default Mode Network

The DMN is a group of interconnected brain regions that become active during periods of rest or when a person is not engaged in a focused activity or task. It is a process of defaulting to internal thought processes like memory retrieval, daydreaming, or when you are mind-wandering (Brandman et al., 2021).

Of significance for those experiencing PTSD is the role that DMN plays in supporting self-referential processes, or those functions that allow us to gather insight about our own mental and physical state (Terpou et al., 2020). For those experiencing PTSD, the DMN has been found to exhibit reduced functional connectivity. This disruption to functional connectivity can lead to intrusive thoughts, difficulty regulating self-referential thinking, and a disrupted sense of self conditions associated with the trauma experienced (Averill et al., 2024). With PTSD, the DMN may become "stuck" on trauma-related memories, causing re-experiencing symptoms. Growing evidence suggests that alterations within or between constituent DMN structures may relate to avoidant, dissociative, and intrusive symptoms of PTSD (Akiki et al., 2017).

Emotional Regulation and the Limbic System

Emotional dysregulation is a core symptom of PTSD and manifests as intense emotional responses, avoidance behaviors, and difficulty identifying or expressing emotions (American Psychiatric Association, 2022). Emotional dysregulation is believed to be the source of the hypervigilance, hyper-arousal, enhanced startle response, irritability, generalization of fear, and avoidance of trauma reminders that characterize the experience of PTSD (Frewen & Lanius, 2006).

Emotional regulation refers to how individuals influence their emotions, including their experience, intensity, and expression (McRae & Gross, 2020). Trauma is believed to interfere with the prefrontal cortex's control over emotional regulation and decision-making (Bolwerk et al., 2014). When the prefrontal cortex is interrupted, the brain's inability to process emotions effectively appears overwhelmed, leading to dysregulation and distress (van der Kolk, 2015).

Engaging in art-making activities can be a conduit for emotional regulation. Research using neuroimaging techniques has demonstrated that creative activities can activate the parasympathetic nervous system, reducing stress and promoting a sense of calm (Kaimal et al., 2016). It has also been shown that engaging in creative activities can reduce activity in the amygdala, the brain's fear and stress center, promoting relaxation and emotional stability, as well as increasing the connectivity between the amygdala and the prefrontal cortex, which helps mitigate hyperarousal and facilitates emotional regulation (Bolwerk et al., 2014). Furthermore, art-making enhances the release of dopamine and serotonin, neurotransmitters associated with mood regulation, pleasure, and reward processing, which can counteract the anhedonia (i.e., loss of interest, pleasure, or motivation) often experienced by trauma survivors (Zaidel, 2014).

Processing and Storing Memories

PTSD alters the brain's structures and functioning and often disrupts the integration of explicit or declarative memories (i.e., consciously recalled) and implicit memories (i.e., those unconsciously stored) (Damis, 2022). The experience of trauma is believed to contribute to symptoms of intrusive thoughts and images because memories of traumatic experiences are consolidated and firmly established within the first few hours of an event. It is as if the traumatic experience is "locked in." Failure to integrate sensory and fear-related memories with explicit autobiographical, declarative memories of experiences and episodes that have occurred in a client's life (Damis, 2022) invites the experience of intrusive memories and re-experiencing of traumatic events in the "now" (Kleim et al., 2008).

Two brain centers, the amygdala and hippocampus, are central to the processing and storing emotional traumatic memories. The amygdala is a central processing center for emotions, and the hippocampus is the part of the brain responsible for memory. With PTSD, trauma hyperactivates the amygdala while impairing hippocampal function, thus preventing the processing and contextualization of the traumatic event and failing to move the experience into explicit memory (van der Kolk, 2015).

The processing and storage of traumatic experience into one's long-term memory requires coordination of the brain's two hemispheres. The right hemisphere actively processes sensory input and emotions (Schore, 2012), whereas the left hemisphere is associated with logic, analytical thinking, and sequential processing. Research (e.g., Saar-Ashkenazy et al., 2016) suggests that the connections between the two hemispheres may be impaired, reducing coordination. Trauma's impact on the amygdala, hippocampus, and coordination of hemispheres ultimately results in the individual struggling with re-experiencing and perpetuating their distress.

Neuroplasticity and Reconsolidation of Traumatic Memories

While trauma can affect the structure and functioning of one's brain, the brain can also reorganize itself, forming new neural connections. This neuroplasticity allows an individual who has experienced trauma to rewire their brain to better cope with the trauma (Bremner et al., 2008). These new neural pathways can bypass the areas impaired by the trauma, allowing the individual to regain coping ability (Kays et al., 2012).

Art therapy has been found to stimulate neuroplastic changes in the brain's organization and neuronal connectivity (Sun et al., 2020). Engaging in creative art activities activates both hemispheres of the brain, particularly the right hemisphere, which is responsible for processing emotions and sensory input (Schore, 2012). Integration between the left (i.e., the analytical) and right (i.e., intuitive) hemispheres of the brain allows for the complete processing and storage of traumatic experiences in long-term memory.

Art therapy and artistic materials can trigger emotions, enabling access to traumatic memories, even those inaccessible through verbal communication (Hass-Cohen & Carr, 2008; Maddox et al., 2024). Art therapy is hypothesized to bring order to traumatic experiences by creating links to nonverbal memories so that dissociated memories may be organized and processed meaningfully (Gantt & Tinnin, 2009). In this way, art therapy helps clients access memories, reconsolidate and integrate them, and reduce trauma-related memories and PTSD symptomology (Barnett & Vasiu, 2024; Schnitzer et al., 2021).

Art therapy can help the client explore alternative perspectives and meanings and reframe the traumatic experience. It allows clients to experience a nonverbal outlet for processing emotions and memories. Creating symbolic representations of trauma can transform distressing imagery into empowering narratives, which is particularly beneficial for individuals with complex trauma or for those who find engaging with their emotions difficult (see Case Illustration 3.1).

CASE ILLUSTRATION 3.1 **That Is What I Need to Remember**

Client Background: Alexa, a 31-year-old trauma physician and first responder, was diagnosed with PTSD following her involvement with a multiple-car pileup in which three children under the age of 3 were crushed and burned. Alexa was the first medical professional on the scene and the first to discover the charred bodies in the back of an SUV. It was an experience unlike any that she'd ever had before.

Since the event, which occurred eight weeks before her session with, the therapist, Alexa, experienced intrusive thoughts and images of the dead children. "Every night I am awakened by seeing those poor little children—their crushed and burned bodies. I cannot shake the images and the fact that I did nothing. I was helpless in rescuing these children."

During the initial session, several goals were established, including helping her gain a more accurate perspective on the event and her role, and foster a sense of self-empowerment, agency, and control.

Medium Selection in Art Therapy

Alexa was introduced to various art materials, including drawing pencils, pastels, acrylic paints, clay, charcoal, and collage materials, and invited to select what she might want to use. However, she had difficulty selecting. The therapist reminded her of her goals to gain a more accurate perspective and acquire a sense of agency over her symptoms. With that as a focus, Rosalie opted to make a collage.

Rosalie was directed to make a collage reflecting anything that she wished. While expressing a lack of clarity about what she would make, she began gathering article headlines, magazine pictures, and samples of colored cloth. Halfway through her creation, she stopped and began to cry. "This is horrible, it's macabre, look, children upside down, parts from their pictures, everything is chaotic, black and red ... I cannot stand it." As she stared and cried, the therapist gently and supportively reminded her that she was the artist and invited her to continue. With the therapist's encouragement and support, she rearranged some of the material, reducing the number of pictures she ripped to create truncated body parts, opening up space on the art paper. With a third of the paper now free of material, she placed a picture of two adults hugging along with a cut-out picture of two hands gently holding a child's head and face.

Looking at the new configuration, and crying, she shared, "I can still see those children—three little ones, but I forgot there were four. There were four. I forgot. I was able to push the back of the seat and get her out. I remember I gave her CPR, and when she began to breathe, I cradled her in my hands. I can remember seeing her open her eyes, beautiful brown eyes. I need to focus on her ... and the others I helped that day, not those I could not save. That is what I need to remember."

Providing Psychological Distance

Psychological distance refers to the ability to separate oneself from emotionally charged experiences. This process allows one to reflect and take perspective (Davis et al., 2011). Given that for many individuals with

PTSD, their traumatic memories are overwhelming, assisting them in experiencing some psychological distance is essential for effective re-framing of the experience.

Art therapy, as a nonverbal modality, provides clients with a sense of psychological distance from the trauma. This allows them to express complex emotions and experiences without relying on words, which can feel inadequate or retraumatizing (Hass-Cohen & Carr, 2008). The use of artistic materials triggers emotions, enabling access to traumatic memories and helping clients explore them safely, step-by-step (Collie et al., 2006).

With art therapy, clients can choose the level of detail and intensity with which they engage with their trauma. This controlled exposure helps them approach painful memories gradually, reducing the risk of retraumatization (Gantt & Tinnin, 2009). Further, the fact that clients are provided the choice of materials, colors, and content fosters a sense of agency that contrasts with the helplessness often associated with trauma. The sense of safety and agency experienced with art therapy helps clients gain distance from overwhelming emotions, facilitating reflection and insight (Malchiodi, 2020) (see Case Illustration 3.2).

CASE ILLUSTRATION 3.2 Hard Not to Smash

John, a former military service member, currently unemployed, was referred to therapy by his primary physician after an incident where he shouted at a stranger in a grocery store for what he later described as a "minor inconvenience."

John served two tours of duty in a combat zone where he experienced life-threatening situations and witnessed the deaths of close friends. He reports feeling "on edge all the time," experiencing intense anger without apparent provocation, and regretting his actions afterward. John avoids public places when possible and has noticed growing isolation from family and friends. His explosive anger has strained relationships, including with his ex-wife and six-year-old son.

When queried about his anger and explosive outbursts, John avoided the topic and attempted to minimize the experience, "It is no big deal. So I get a little pissed, once in a while." When the therapist invited John to go further, he became agitated and demonstrated the anger outburst that concerned his friends and family. He yelled at the therapist:

> Look you have no friggin' clue what it's like over there. You have been on your toes 24/7. There is no going easy or going slow. You have to be like a viper ready to strike—or else you will suffer the blow.

John was quick to apologize for the outburst.

> I am sorry, doc. It is just really hard. I spent years developing this style. It worked over there, but I know it has no place here. But I just think it is part of me. I don't like talking about it.

Given the expressed frustration and sense of hopelessness about gaining control over his outburst, and the apparent discomfort talking up his experience, the therapist engaged in a creative nonverbal activity.

After explaining the nature and potential value of therapeutically engaging with creative materials, the therapist gave John clay and invited him to shape it into something that represented how he felt at that moment. With some initial reluctance, John began to roll the clay into a ball. He held the clay for a few moments, threw it on the table, and smashed it ... flattening it out.

The therapist allowed John to repeat the process of balling—throwing and aggressively smashing the clay. He then invited John to try something different. He asked John to create the ball as before, but this time, rather than aggressively smashing it, he would place it on the table and gently smooth and flatten the clay, as if making a pizza. This process was repeated, and the therapist invited John to discuss the experience.

John was quick to note: "That was hard. I'm unsure why I kept smashing the ball—I felt like I couldn't control it. I just felt so angry and tense. But then, when you asked me to smooth it out, like a pizza, I felt silly about beating it up. The second time I did it, I looked at what I was doing and realized I was in control. I realized I could smash it, but I didn't have to. It was my choice."

The freedom and control provided to clients in art therapy encourage their engagement. The artwork created provides a visible and tangible expression of the client's experience and provides the needed distance from the associated memories that allows the client to share and process the meaning of the artwork (Heijman et al., 2024).

Facilitating Disclosure and Discussion

As demonstrated in Case Illustration 3.2, one of art therapy's unique strengths in trauma recovery is its nonverbal nature. Many trauma survivors struggle to articulate their experiences through words due to avoidance, dissociation, or limited access to explicit memories (van der Kolk, 2000).

Art-making provides an alternative pathway for expression, enabling clients to communicate complex emotions and memories without relying on verbal language. Art therapy can help suppressed, unconscious, or avoided material to be accessed and enable clients to gain a broader perspective to be considered (Lobban, 2018).

Talking about traumatic events can sometimes exacerbate distress, particularly when survivors feel unready to confront their narratives (Gantt & Tinnin, 2009). Art therapy uses creative materials and processes as mediators to help clients externalize and gain emotional distance from the trauma (Heijman et al., 2024).

Art therapy allows individuals to explore their experiences at their own pace, fostering a sense of safety and autonomy. Moreover, art-making's visual and tactile nature can bypass cognitive defenses, allowing deeper emotional processing (McCarthy, n.d.).

Case Illustration 3.3 highlights the value of art therapy in facilitating a client's emotional safety and ability to reflect upon and process a traumatic experience that is too difficult to discuss.

CASE ILLUSTRATION 3.3 Hiding for Safety

Rhea, eight years old, was referred to therapy by social services following a traumatic event where she witnessed domestic violence at home. Since the incident, she has become withdrawn, exhibited symptoms of anxiety, and struggled to express her emotions verbally.

During the initial sessions, Rhea was reluctant to speak about her experiences and would either completely shut down or attempt to divert the conversation to another topic. Throughout the interaction with the therapist, she exhibited hypervigilance and would tense in response to sudden noises, indicative of her heightened arousal and distress. Her inability to articulate her feelings suggested a need for a nonverbal therapeutic modality.

The therapist provided Rhea with crayons, markers, colored pencils, and clay. Rhea was encouraged to play with the art materials and create anything she wished. Initially, she created somewhat abstract animal figures gathered in what appeared to be a wooded area.

The therapist was supportive and slowly introduced prompts to explore Rhea's feelings. The initial conversation focused on identifying the animals, what they were doing, and which animal Rhea (and the therapist) would like to be. The focus on the drawing and the therapist's nonjudgmental nature appeared to provide the safety Rhea needed to begin to relax.

The therapist invited Rhea to include herself in the drawings. Encouraged, she added a tree to what was beginning to look like a forest with animals. At the base of the tree, she colored a dark round hole from which she added two eyes staring out. Returning to a discussion about the animals and adding the tree and eyes, the therapist had Rhea explain that the eyes belonged to a girl playing hide-and-seek.

The identification of an anonymous girl and the context of the game appeared to provide the safety from which Rhea could begin to share her need to "hide." This need for safety and self-protection became the focus of upcoming sessions, with the therapist assisting Rhea to experience the safety and control she desired.

From Knowledge to Application

One need not have experienced trauma or prolonged stress to experience the therapeutic benefits of art and creative activities. You have read about the value of art therapy in providing emotional distance and safety, assisting with reconsolidating memories and reframing emotional experiences. Exercise 3.1 invites you to experience the positive effects of art and creative activities as you explore an emotion or memory of interest.

EXERCISE 3.1 Exploring Emotion and Memory

This exercise is designed to help you experience the therapeutic benefits of engaging in art and creative activities to explore an emotion or memory of interest.

Part 1: Preparation

- Create a calm, inviting space that provides a sense of safety and privacy.
- Gather various art supplies (e.g., paper, markers, colored pencils, paint, clay).
- Choose an emotion or memory that feels significant to you today. This could be something you find challenging or want to explore.

Part 2: The Creative Process

- Select a medium (drawing, painting, sculpting) and the art materials you will use to represent how this feels to you visually.
- Remember, this is not graded or judged. Allow yourself to get into the process of creating.

Part 3: Reflection

- Take a few moments to observe your creation.
  - What do you notice about what you created?
  - Does anything about your creation surprise you?
  - How did it feel to express your emotion or memory through art?
  - Did you experience new insights or feelings as you engaged with the materials?
  - What message does this creation or the experience of creating it leave you with today?

The Takeaway

Creative experiences and art therapy provide a unique and practical approach to treating individuals experiencing PTSD. Art therapy creates psychological distance, allowing clients to externalize their trauma into visual forms that are more manageable to reflect upon and analyze.

Through symbolic representation, clients can explore emotions and experiences in a less threatening way. This fosters gradual engagement with the trauma and reduces the risk of retraumatization. By integrating art therapy into trauma treatment, clinicians can harness the power of creativity to facilitate nonverbal expression, emotional regulation, and neurologically informed healing.

Keystones

- While traditional psychological interventions such as CBT and exposure therapies are effective, art therapy is increasingly recognized for its unique benefits, particularly for individuals with PTSD who struggle with verbal expression.
- Art therapy activates brain regions like the prefrontal cortex and the default mode network (DMN), fostering mental adaptability.
- Art therapy supports emotional regulation by activating the parasympathetic nervous system, reducing stress, and enhancing the release of neurotransmitters (dopamine and serotonin).
- Neuroimaging shows reduced amygdala activity and increased connectivity with the prefrontal cortex, mitigating hyperarousal.
- Art therapy provides psychological distance, allowing clients to externalize and process emotions safely and gradually.
- Through symbolic representation and creative reframing, clients can access, reconsolidate, and transform traumatic memories into coherent, empowering narratives.
- Art therapy enables trauma survivors to communicate complex emotions and experiences that may be inaccessible through verbal language.

ADDITIONAL RESOURCES

Christopher, G. (2024). Healing trauma and building empathy through art therapy. *International Journal of Art Therapy, 29*(4), 182–183. https://doi.org/10.1080/17454832.2024.2418226

King, J. L., & Strang, C. E. (Eds.). (2024). *Art therapy and the neuroscience of trauma* (2nd ed.). Taylor and Francis.

Malhotra, B., Jones, L. C., Spooner, H., Levy, C., Kaimal, G., & Williamson, J. B. (2024). A conceptual framework for a neurophysiological basis of art therapy for PTSD. *Frontiers in Human Neuroscience, 18,* 1351757. https://doi.org/10.3389/fnhum.2024.1351757

REFERENCES

Akiki, T. J., Averill, C. L., & Abdallah, C. G. (2017). A network-based neurobiological model of PTSD: evidence from structural and functional neuroimaging studies. *Current Psychiatry Reports, 19*(11), 1–10.

American Psychological Association. (2025). *Clinical practice guideline for the treatment of PTSD.* American Psychological Association. https://www.apa.org/ptsd-guideline/ptsd.pdf 2025).

American Psychiatric Association. (2022). *Diagnostic and statistical manual of mental disorders* (5th ed., text rev.). American Psychiatric Association. https://doi.org/10.1176/appi.books.9780890425787

Averill, C. L., Averill, L. A., Akiki, T. J., Fouda, S., Krystal, J. H., & Abdallah, C. G. (2024). Findings of PTSD-specific deficits in default mode network strength following a mild experimental stressor. *NPP—Digital Psychiatry and Neuroscience, 2,* 9. https://doi.org/10.1038/s44277-024-00011-y

Barnett, K. S., & Vasiu, F. (2024). How the arts heal: A review of the neural mechanisms behind the therapeutic effects of creative arts on mental and physical health. *Frontiers in Behavioral Neuroscience, 18,* 1422361. https://doi.org/10.3389/fnbeh.2024.1422361

Bolwerk, A., Mack-Andrick, J., Lang, F. R., Dörfler, A., & Maihöfner, C. (2014). How art changes your brain: differential effects of visual art production and cognitive art evaluation on functional brain connectivity. *PloS One, 9*(7), e101035. https://doi.org/10.1371/journal.pone.0101035

Brandman, T., Malach, R. & Simony, E. (2021). The surprising role of the default mode network in naturalistic perception. *Communications Biology, 4,* 79. https://doi.org/10.1038/s42003-020-01602-z

Bremner J. D. (2007). Neuroimaging in posttraumatic stress disorder and other stress-related disorders. *Neuroimaging Clinics of North America, 17*(4), 523–538. https://doi.org/10.1016/j.nic.2007.07.003

Bremner, J. D., Elzinga, B., Schmahl, C., & Vermetten, E. (2008). Structural and functional plasticity of the human brain in posttraumatic stress disorder. *Progress in Brain Research, 167,* 171–186. https://doi.org/10.1016/S0079-6123(07)67012-5

Collie, K., Malchiodi, C., Backos, A., & Spiegel, D. (2006). Art therapy for combat-related PTSD: Recommendations for research and practice. *Art Therapy, 23*(4), 157–164.

Damis L. F. (2022). The role of implicit memory in the development and recovery from trauma-related disorders. *NeuroSci,* 3(1), 63–88. https://doi.org/10.3390/neurosci3010005

Davis, J. I., Gross, J. J., & Ochsner, K. N. (2011). Psychological distance and emotional experience: What you see is what you get. *Emotion, 11*(2), 438–444. https://doi.org/10.1037/a0021783

Frewen, P. A., & Lanius, R. A. (2006). Toward a psychobiology of posttraumatic self-dysregulation: Reexperiencing, hyperarousal, dissociation, and emotional numbing. *Annals of the New York Academy of Sciences, 1071*(1), 110–124.

Gantt, L., & Tinnin, L. W. (2009). Support for a neurobiological view of trauma with implications for art therapy. *The Arts in Psychotherapy, 36*(3), 148–153. https://doi.org/10.1016/j.aip.2008.12.005

Haeyen, S., & Wanten, F. (2024). Effectiveness of Trauma-Focused Art Therapy (TFAT) for psychological trauma: A mixed method single case study. *The Arts in Psychotherapy, 91,* 102218. https://www.sciencedirect.com/science/article/pii/S0197455624001035

Hass-Cohen, N., & Carr, R. (2008). *Art therapy and clinical neuroscience.* Jessica Kingsley Publishers.

Heijman, J., Wouters, H., Schouten, K. A., & Haeyen, S. (2024). Effectiveness of trauma-focused art therapy (TFAT) for psychological trauma: Study protocol of a multiple-baseline single-case experimental design. *BMJ Open, 14*(1), e081917. https://do.org/10.1136/bmjopen-2023-081917

Kaimal, G., Ray, K., & Muniz, J. (2016). Reduction of cortisol levels and participants' responses following art making. *Art Therapy: Journal of the American Art Therapy Association,* 33(2), 74–80. https://doi.org/10.1080/07421656.2016.1166832

Kays, J. L., Hurley, R. A., & Taber, K. H. (2012). The Dynamic Brain: Neuroplasticity and Mental Health. *The Journal of Neuropsychiatry and Clinical Neurosciences, 24*(2), 118–124. https://doi.org/10.1176/appi.neuropsych.12050109

Kleim, B., Wallott, F., & Ehlers, A. (2008). Are trauma memories disjointed from other autobiographical memories in posttraumatic stress disorder? An experimental investigation. *Behavioural and Cognitive Psychotherapy, 36*(2), 221–234. https://doi.org/10.1017/S1352465807004080

Lobban, J. (2018). Bypassing the sentinel. In J. Lobban (Ed.), *Art therapy with military veterans: Trauma and the image* (pp. 152–166). Routledge. https://doi.org/10.4324/9781315564197-10

Maddox, G. A., Bodner, G. E., Christian, M. W., & Williamson, P. (2024). On the effectiveness of visual arts therapy for traumatic experiences: A systematic review and meta-analysis. *Clinical Psychology & Psychotherapy, 31*(4): e3041. https://doi.org/10.1002/cpp.3041

Malchiodi, C. A. (2020). *Trauma and expressive arts therapy: Brain, body, and imagination in the healing process.* Guilford Press.

McCarthy, C. (n.d.). *Art therapy as a method of regulating psychological defenses.* Greater Chicago Art Therapy. Retrieved https://greaterchicagoarttherapy.com/art-therapy-blog/exploring-the-role-of-art-therapy-in-reducing-treatment-inhibiting-psychological-defense-mechanisms#:~:text=While%20conventional%20therapies%20and%20medical,the%20exploration%20of%20defended%20material.

McRae, K., & Gross, J. J. (2020). Emotion regulation. *Emotion, 20*(1), 1–9. https://doi.org/10.1037/emo0000703

Saar-Ashkenazy, R., Veksler, R., Guez, J., Jacob, Y., Shelef, I., Shalev, H., Friedman, A., & Cohen, J. E. (2016). Breakdown of inter-hemispheric connectivity is associated with posttraumatic symptomatology and memory impairment. *PloS One, 11*(2), e0144766. https://doi.org/10.1371/journal.pone.0144766

Schnitzer, G., Holttum, S., & Huet, V. (2021). A systematic literature review of the impact of art therapy upon post-traumatic stress disorder. *International Journal of Art Therapy, 26*(4), 147–160. https://doi.org/10.1080/17454832.2021.1910719

Schore, A. N. (2012). *The science of the art of psychotherapy.* W. W. Norton.

Sun, J., Zhang, Q., Li, Y., Meng, J., Chen, Q., Yang, W., Wei, D., & Qiu, J. (2020). Plasticity of the resting-state brain: Static and dynamic functional connectivity change induced by divergent thinking training. *Brain Imaging and Behavior, 14*(5), 1498–1506.

Terpou, B. A., Densmore, M., Théberge, J., Frewen, P., McKinnon, M. C., Nicholson, A. A., & Lanius, R. A. (2020). The hijacked self: Disrupted functional connectivity between the periaqueductal gray and the default mode network in posttraumatic stress disorder using dynamic causal modeling. *NeuroImage: Clinical, 27,* 102345. https://doi.org/10.1016/j.nicl.2020.102345

van der Kolk B. (2000). Posttraumatic stress disorder and the nature of trauma. *Dialogues in Clinical Neuroscience, 2*(1), 7–22. https://doi.org/10.31887/DCNS.2000.2.1/bvdkolk

van der Kolk, B. A. (2015). *The body keeps the score: Brain, mind, and body in the healing of trauma.* Viking.

Zaidel, D. W. (2014). Creativity, brain, and art: Biological and neurological considerations. *Frontiers in Human Neuroscience, 8,* 389. https://doi.org/10.3389/fnhum.2014.00389

PART II

Art Therapy in Practice

CHAPTER 4

Art Therapy Models and Protocols for Trauma Treatment

The trauma-focused psychotherapies jointly recommended by the APA guidelines (American Psychological Association, 2017) and the VA/DoD (Veterans Affairs/Department of Defense) guideline (Card, 2017) are prolonged exposure (Foa et al., 2008) and cognitive processing therapy (CPT; Resick et al., 2016). These treatments have been tested using randomly assigned control designs in patients with complex presentations and comorbidities.

While proven effective, research has shown that more than one-third of clients do not benefit from these interventions, especially those with poor verbal memory and/or emotional difficulties with talking about traumatic experiences (Bradley et al., 2005). For this population, art therapy can provide adjunctive treatment to facilitate improved trauma processing.

Several art therapy protocols and approaches exist for treating trauma, each offering unique techniques and theoretical foundations. These protocols typically integrate evidence-based principles of trauma recovery, including the three-phase approach of stabilization, processing, and integration (Herman, 1997). It is in the phase of processing that the various theoretical models diverge employing their unique orientation and interventions to assist the client in reframing and processing the experience.

The current chapter reviews three approaches: trauma-focused art therapy, art therapy trauma protocol, and focusing-oriented art therapy. Upon completion of the chapter, readers will be able to:

1. Describe the methodology and techniques each approach employs;
2. Compare the techniques employed by each approach in assisting clients in processing and reintegrating their traumatic experiences.

Trauma-Focused Art Therapy (TFAT)

TFAT emerged as practitioners sought to adapt evidence-based trauma interventions to diverse populations, including children, adolescents, and adults, in a way that enhanced engagement and outcomes (Chapman et al., 2001). TFAT draws heavily from trauma-focused cognitive-behavioral therapy (TF-CBT), which emphasizes addressing trauma through a structured framework of psychoeducation, emotional processing, and cognitive restructuring (Cohen et al., 2006). Unlike traditional TF-CBT, TFAT incorporates nonverbal, creative modalities to help clients access and process trauma that may not be accessible through verbal means.

TFAT has demonstrated efficacy in diverse populations, including children, refugees, and military veterans. Research highlights its ability to reduce PTSD symptoms, improve emotional regulation, and enhance resilience (Kapitan, 2018; Schouten et al., 2015).

Methodologies in Trauma-Focused Art Therapy

Trauma-focused art therapy protocol is a short-term trauma-focused intervention. The protocol includes eleven weekly sessions of 60 minutes and consists of three phases: (1) stabilization and symptom reduction, (2) trauma-processing, and (3) integration.

Phase I. Stabilization and Symptom Reduction

The first phase consists of four sessions focusing the client on the present to reduce the client's experience of stress and arousal and thus increase their sense of control. This stage involves working toward internal and external safety for the client. It begins by building a therapeutic alliance and relationship with the therapist so the client feels safe to move forward. Discussing a client's memories is not a focus during this phase (Herman, 1997).

Clients will be invited to create grounding symbols or mandalas that represent safety. In addition to using a color chart to express their emotions visually, clients during this first phase will draw or sculpt a "safe container" that symbolizes emotional boundaries (Henderson et al., 2007; Schouten et al., 2019).

Once the client appears stable, they will be assisted in accessing memories and directed to make a list of five items related to the memories. When clients can achieve this task by listing positive and traumatic memories without being overwhelmed, the therapy moves to the next phase.

Phase II. Trauma-Processing

When safety and stabilization have been achieved, trauma therapy moves into the second stage, which addresses the more profound impact of trauma by processing and integrating the traumatic experiences. The second phase is trauma processing and consists of five sessions (sessions 5–9) focused on the present and past. It becomes a time of grief and mourning (Herman, 1997) as clients begin to deconstruct negative beliefs that have formed within them as a result of the trauma and work to develop positive schemas or beliefs (McCann & Pearlman, 1990; Roth et al., 1997).

Throughout this phase, the focus is on assisting the client in accessing and expressing traumatic and positive memories. To externalize traumatic memories, clients may be asked to create a visual narrative or timeline. They will use metaphors, such as storms, clouds, and broken objects, in their drawings.

Following sessions in which a traumatic memory is expressed in the client's artwork, the therapist guides the client to experience relaxation. Clients are also guided through a gradual exposure technique to depict their trauma in stages from less distressing to challenging. In the last session of this phase, clients retrieve a positive memory to express in the artwork. This sets the stage for the final phase of treatment.

Phase III. Integration and Meaning-Making

The third stage of recovery focuses on reconnecting with people, meaningful activities, and other aspects of life. The integration and meaning-making phase consists of two sessions (sessions 10–11), focusing on cognitive restructuring and integrating the trauma narrative into a broader life story.

During this phase, clients transform the memories and emotions expressed during the previous phases into new artwork that reflects integration and forward-looking perspectives. Clients may create before-and-after art pieces that symbolize their journey and depict their future selves, focusing on hope, strength, and goals. Case Illustration 4.1 provides an abbreviated view of this protocol.

CASE ILLUSTRATION 4.1 Amara as Superhero

Amara (pseudonym) is 10 years old and is in therapy following her removal from her parents' custody and her home. Social services intervened in what had become a potentially life-endangering situation.

Amara had witnessed repeated episodes of domestic violence in her home, often involving police interventions. She is currently experiencing symptoms of hypervigilance, nightmares, and difficulty expressing emotions.

Amara was resistant to all invitations to talk about her experience, and as such, the therapist introduced her to the idea of engaging in creative activities and art. The goals of the therapy were to help reduce Amara's PTSD symptoms by helping her process and reframe traumatic memories and establish a sense of safety and empowerment. The approach taken was that of trauma-focused art therapy.

Phase 1: Safety and Stabilization

During the initial session, the therapist invited Amara to draw her "safe place." Using colored pencils, she drew a treehouse, almost hidden behind leaves on the tree. The house had flowers in boxes on the windowsills and what she described as "butterflies" all around the front. Creating the picture and focusing the discussion on it, rather than her experiences at home, helped Amara to experience some grounding and reduction of her initial anxiety. It also worked as a stimulant for Amara to share her desire to be safe.

Phase 2: Trauma Narrative and Processing

The sessions throughout the second phase of treatment focused on the creation of a timeline, one reflecting her traumatic experiences. Amara used different shapes and colors to represent the events, continuing to avoid direct discussion.

Throughout the sessions, Amara began expanding the timeline to include positive experiences. Externalizing her memories, both those she called "yucky" and some of the positive experiences, gave her the psychological distance needed to begin verbalizing her experience at home and her feelings of fear and sadness.

Phase 3: Integration and Resilience-Building

The final sessions focused on helping Amara recognize her ability (power) to protect herself and reinforce her resilience. The therapist was able to engage Amara in this reflection by having her first create a self-portrait in an image of a superhero (see Figure 4.1).

FIGURE 4.1 Amara as Superhero[1]

Outcome

By the end of the 12-week intervention, Amara demonstrated significant reductions in PTSD symptoms, including improved sleep, decreased anxiety, and greater emotional expression. Her artwork was a therapeutic tool and a tangible representation of her healing journey.

[1] All the art included in this text reflects actual clients' work. They have, however, been modified by ChatGPT 4.0 to protect the client's anonymity.

Art Therapy Trauma Protocol (ATTP)

The art therapy trauma protocol (Talwar, 2007) provides a straightforward, step-by-step approach designed to address the nonverbal, somatic memory of traumatized clients. The protocol is influenced by Shapiro's (2007) adaptive information processing system (AIPS), which proposes that each individual has the innate ability to construct adaptive resolutions to negative experiences and to integrate positive and negative emotional schemata using right- and left-brain methods.

ATTP incorporates psychoeducation, gradual exposure, and post-traumatic growth principles into a creative, client-centered approach (Chapman et al., 2001). By engaging the right hemisphere of the brain, which processes nonverbal experiences, ATTP facilitates access to implicit memories and supports their integration into the client's conscious narrative (van der Kolk, 2014). ATTP's effectiveness aligns with trauma-informed care principles, emphasizing safety, empowerment, and client-centered practice.

The Core of Art Therapy Trauma Protocol (ATTP)

The art therapy trauma protocol is a structured approach to trauma treatment that integrates evidence-based principles of trauma recovery, including Herman's (1997) three-phase approach of stabilization, processing, and integration. The therapist's attunement to the client's emotional state guides each phase, ensuring the process remains supportive and nonretraumatizing.

The protocol emphasizes the engagement of the brain's left and right hemispheres. Clients will be asked to draw or paint with dominant and nondominant hands and even walk back and forth while creating their artwork to engage bilateral stimulation and dual processing (Omaha, 2004). The bilateral stimulation through art-making engages the prefrontal cortex to integrate, plan, and develop a narrative of the memories' beginning, middle, and end in the hippocampus (Talwar, 2007).

Stabilization Phase

Just as trauma-focused art therapy attempts to establish the client's safety during its first phase of treatment, ATTP starts its protocol by engaging clients to create visual representations of safe places and designing and decorating "containment" boxes to store distressing thoughts and memories metaphorically. In addition to these grounding exercises, ATTP helps clients develop emotion wheels or feeling thermometers to help them identify and regulate emotional states.

Once safety and stabilization are established, the client will be asked to suspend all thoughts and associations and begin painting. When the client is finished, they are asked to put into words the dominant emotion associated with the painting or element of the painting. In Case Illustration 4.2, we are introduced to Nicole. Nicole was viciously attacked by a coworker, which left her blind in one eye and facially scared. Her first drawing (see Figure 4.2a) reflected her desire to hide, to disappear.

CASE ILLUSTRATION 4.2 Nicole—Scarred

Nicole, a 33-year-old financial adviser, presented for therapy following a vicious attack by a coworker, which left her blind in one eye and facially scared. The experience traumatized Nicole, and she currently experiences sleep disturbance and flashbacks and is avoiding all social contact (including returning to work). When invited to create her art, she drew a black stick figure, head down, with hands covering her face. When asked to describe her drawing, she stated, "I wish I could disappear—I am horrible and completely inadequate to care for myself. I wish I could disappear ... fade into the dark" (see Figure 4.2a).

FIGURE 4.2A Fade into the Dark

The therapist working with Nicole was employing a trauma-focused cognitive processing approach as the primary treatment modality, with the creative activities serving in a supplemental role to facilitate conversation around difficult topics and monitor progress. At the end of their fifth session, the therapist presented Nicole with art supplies and invited her to draw what she was feeling. As she had done in each previous session, Nicole began to draw a self-portrait. This time, however, rather than attempting to draw a "hidden" self, she drew a facial portrait. In the image, rather than a stick figure without a face, she showed a frontal view of her face, with multiple red lines indicating cuts and scars and a right eye which was blackened out, as missing (see Figure 4.2b). The figure continues to have scars and a look that she described as "on guard."

FIGURE 4.2B Emerging as a Person

Throughout the final ten weeks of therapy, Nicole continued to gain confidence and feelings of empowerment. She no longer had flashbacks or a need to hide and avoid friends and coworkers. Her self-portraits took on a more attractive, smiling appearance. Her final drawing included makeup, a new hairstyle, and a bejeweled eye patch (see Figure 4.2c).

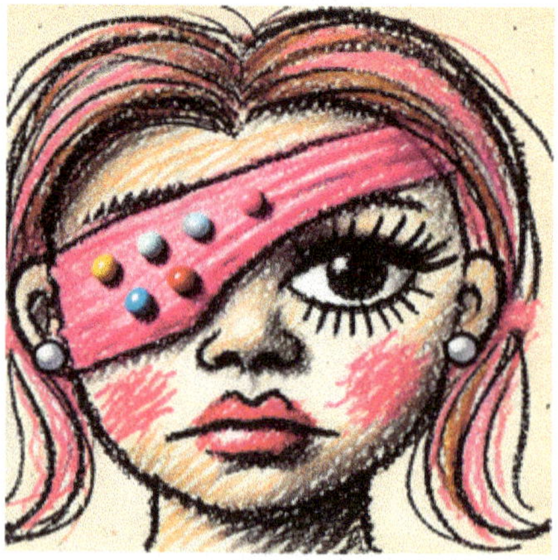

FIGURE 4.2C Acceptance and Growth

Trauma Processing Phase

The second phase of ATTP attempts to assist clients in processing and integrating traumatic memories in a manageable and controlled manner. The client is asked to create an image using their nondominant hand. While painting with the nondominant hand, the client is asked to concentrate on the disturbing traumatic memory while keeping the negative cognition and physiological sensation in mind. The client paints the new images and memories as they emerge on a new sheet of paper.

At this stage of therapy, Nicole (Case Illustration 4.2) could begin to step out from the darkness and present herself, as reflected in her frontal facial portrait (Figure 4.2b). This acceptance continued to grow over the subsequent seven sessions.

Integration and Growth Phase

The final phase aims to promote cognitive restructuring and integrate trauma into the client's cohesive life narrative. The client continues painting, switching between dominant and nondominant hands and using a new sheet of paper each time. Thus, the client works through the memory until recalling the traumatic event no longer causes disturbance.

Returning to Nicole (see Case Illustration 4.2), we find that her drawings, which during the processing phase focused on facial detail and emphasized scarring and an eye patch, had evolved to what appeared to be a much more accepting self-perspective (Figure 4.2c).

Focusing-Oriented Art Therapy (FOAT)

Focusing-riented art therapy (FOAT; Rappaport, 2009) is a therapeutic approach that integrates the principles of Eugene Gendlin's (1978) focusing method with art therapy's expressive and healing potential. Focusing allows an individual to know what is being felt even when they cannot understand those feelings.

Focusing-oriented art therapy assists individuals in listening to their inner selves and speaking through emotions rather than about them (Rappaport, 2009). This level of felt sense experience opens a client to new insight and a bodily feeling of release and provides a sense of empowerment in the face of trauma (Klagsbrun & Lennox, 2012).

Laury Rappaport's six-step FOAT process offers a structured yet flexible framework that allows clients to access and process implicit emotional experiences through art.

Step 1: Clearing a Space

The first step in FOAT is to create a mental and emotional space for focusing. Clients are guided to identify and temporarily set aside overwhelming concerns, enabling a more centered state for exploration (Gendlin, 1978; Rappaport, 2009). Consider the case of a first-year elementary schoolteacher, Grace, who has been traumatized by observing the death of one of her students, who had a seizure in class and died. She began the session by drawing a large, chaotic swirl of blackness that indicated both her depression and emotional turmoil. After acknowledging her feelings of anger, helplessness, and depression, she modified the picture to include a center swirl of yellow, which she labeled "a ray of light and hope," which she continued to hold onto (see Figure 4.3). She took the picture and physically set it aside to clear space both on the table and in her mind.

FIGURE 4.3 Hope in Darkness

Step 2: Choosing an Issue to Focus on

Once the space has been cleared, the client is invited to check in to see what issue they may want to focus on. In this second step, clients tune into the body's felt sense—a holistic, preverbal awareness of a problem or situation. Through art, this abstract sensation becomes more tangible. For example, our schoolteacher, Grace, identified a feeling of paralysis as if frozen in time and space.

Step 3: Finding a Handle

In the third step, the client creates a word, phrase, or image that encapsulates the essence of the felt sense. This process bridges the abstract and the explicit. Drawing what they felt inside and creating space to reflect on help develop a greater capacity to feel safe (Rappaport, 2009).

In this case, Grace saw the stick figure and labeled it "impotent." The label assisted the therapist with engaging Grace and her reflections on her feelings of impotence and helplessness in intervening at the time of her student's seizure.

Step 4: Resonating the Handle

In step 4, space is given for the client to double-check if this *handle* feels right within and resonates with it. During this step, something else may arise, and the client would be supported to trust their bodily sense that whatever comes up is essential. This step ensures alignment between the internal experience and the external representation. If another handle, word, or description arises, they are encouraged to feel this handle against their felt sense for a match to describe it. This part of the directive is repeated until the client feels that their handle matches the initial felt sense.

Returning to Grace, we find that she felt intense shame and guilt as she reflected on her stick figure and the impotence label. With this added handle, Grace adjusted the figure so that the head was bowed down and the hands covered the face.

Step 5: Asking

This stage involves assisting the client to develop deeper insight and a closer relationship with the felt sense. The therapist facilitates this inquiry by asking questions such as "What does this [image or sensation] need?" Or the client may be asked to imagine sitting down next to the felt sense of an issue with complete acceptance, compassion, and nonjudgment.

The therapist's questions and directives are intended to help the client separate themselves from the feelings the issue brings up within them and in so doing gain a sense of agency and empowerment (Gendlin, 1978; Klagsbrun & Lennox, 2012; Rappaport, 2009). When clients hold the felt sense with acceptance and compassion, they develop a greater capacity to hold other traumas or issues.

Grace, for example, gazed at her first drawing and shifted her focus from the sizeable chaotic swirl to the light (yellow) in the center (see Figure 4.3). She asked herself: "How do I forgive myself? How do I find a light at the end of this tunnel?"

After reflecting on this, she redrew a stick figure, similar to one that she had labeled as "impotent," one reflecting her intense guilt, but this time the figure was standing upright with her arms wrapped around in a self-hug. Grace identified this image as one of forgiveness, strength, and confidence, and it became a focal point of future sessions. The therapist used the image, contrasting it to the one of guilt, to assist Grace in identifying and challenging her irrational beliefs about her responsibility for her student's death and facilitate cognitive reframing.

Step 6: Receiving

The final step is to accept what the felt sense had to say in response to the questions and welcome these messages deeply with compassion and openness. This step focuses on integrating the insights and changes that emerge.

For Grace, the final step was to accept the grief she experienced, the desire that she could have done more, but at the same time accept that she did all that she was capable of and that the child's medical condition was not something that she created, nor sadly, something that she could have remedy. She concretized her insights by creating a new painting (see Figure 4.4), which she described as her goal "to stand strong, in a warm, calm setting and being both a source for, and a recipient of, the light and love shared with her students."

FIGURE 4.4 Grace Back in the Light of Life

From Knowledge to Application

Eugene Gendlin's (1978) focusing method allows individuals to know what is being felt even when they cannot put those feelings into words. Focusing is not restricted to only cases of trauma or clinical distress.

Focusing, in the form of focusing-oriented art therapy, can assist individuals in listening to their inner selves. Exercise 4.1 invites you to use the steps of focusing-oriented art therapy to engage deeply with your inner self.

EXERCISE 4.1 "Journey to the Felt Sense"

Directions: Focusing is neither restricted nor useful in only cases of trauma or clinical distress. This exercise will allow you to engage deeply with your inner self while integrating the six FOAT steps. Gather the materials needed and follow the directions for each step.

Materials Needed

- Paper or canvas
- Colored pencils, markers, or paints
- Clay or other sculpting materials (optional)
- Comfortable seating or meditation cushions
- A quiet, distraction-free environment

Steps

1. **Clearing a Space**

   Objective: Create a calm, reflective state to identify what is in the mind and body.

   - **Instructions**: Begin with a few minutes of mindfulness or grounding. Close your eyes, take deep breaths, and imagine clearing a space inside yourself. Picture setting aside the "noise" of everyday life.
   - **Art Prompt**: On your paper, draw a circle to represent the "cleared space" and add simple lines, shapes, or colors that represent what remains present within you.

2. **Felt Sense**

   Objective: Connect with the vague, preverbal "felt sense" related to a current life situation or emotion.

   - **Instructions**: Place your hand over your heart or stomach and tune into a situation or feeling that feels important but is not yet clear. Notice sensations, images, or words that arise.
   - **Art Prompt**: Using your chosen medium, create a symbolic representation of this "felt sense." Let the image or shapes emerge naturally.

3. **Finding a Handle**

   Objective: Identify a word, phrase, or symbol that resonates with the felt sense.

   - **Instructions**: Look at your artwork and ask yourself: "What word, phrase, or image matches this feeling?" Let it come intuitively.

- **Art Prompt**: Write or incorporate the handle into your artwork (e.g., a word, symbol, or additional marks that enhance the original drawing).

4. **Resonating**

   Objective: Check if the "handle" matches the felt sense and make adjustments if needed.

   - **Instructions**: Hold the word or symbol in your mind while focusing on your felt sense. Does it fit? If not, allow it to shift or change.
   - **Art Prompt**: Modify your artwork to reflect the deeper clarity of the connection between the handle and the felt sense.

5. **Asking**

   Objective: Inquire into what the felt sense wants or needs to express.

   - **Instructions**: Gently ask the felt sense, "What does this need from me?" or "What would feel right here?"
   - **Art Prompt**: Create a new piece of art or add to your existing artwork to express the response to your inquiry.

6. **Receiving**

   Objective: Accept and honor the insights that arise, whether incomplete or unresolved.

   - **Instructions**: Take a moment to appreciate the process and the message your inner self has shared. Sit with any new clarity or questions.
   - **Art Prompt**: Create a final image to honor the entire journey, or write a short reflection next to your artwork.

Process

Take time to consider your experience and insights that may have emerged. What are your thoughts about employing such a technique with a distressed client? You may find it valuable to discuss your experience and observations with a colleague or classmate.

The Takeaway

Art therapy is a powerful modality for addressing the multifaceted impacts of trauma. There are several art therapy protocols and approaches for treating trauma, each offering unique techniques and theoretical foundations. These protocols typically integrate evidence-based principles of trauma recovery, including Herman's (1997) three-phase approach of stabilization, processing, and integration with unique strategies to process the traumatic experience. By integrating creativity with trauma-informed care principles, these models empower clients to process and heal from traumatic experiences, fostering resilience and growth.

Keystones

- Evidence-based psychotherapies for trauma, such as prolonged exposure or cognitive processing therapy, while recommended for use with those experiencing PTSD, are often not practical for clients with poor verbal memory or difficulties verbalizing trauma.
- Art therapy bridges gaps for clients unable to process trauma verbally, emphasizing creative, client-centered interventions.
- Protocols like TFAT, ATTP, and most protocols for art therapy and trauma recovery incorporate Herman's three-phase stabilization, processing, and integration model.
- Trauma-focused art therapy is unique in its adaption of trauma-focused cognitive behavioral therapy with nonverbal, creative modalities.
- Art therapy trauma protocol integrates bilateral stimulation and nonverbal processing of somatic memories.
- Focusing-oriented art therapy is a six-step protocol that integrates Eugene Gendlin's focusing methods to assist individuals in listening to their inner experiences.

ADDITIONAL RESOURCES

Guzman, L. (2020). *Essential art therapy exercises: Effective techniques to manage anxiety, depression, and PTSD.* Rockridge Press.

King, J. L. (Ed.). (2021). *Art therapy, trauma, and neuroscience.* Routledge.

Malchiodi, C. A. (2020). *Trauma and expressive arts therapy: Brain, body, and imagination in the healing process.* Guilford Press.

REFERENCES

American Psychological Association. (2017). *Clinical practice guideline for the treatment of posttraumatic stress disorder (PTSD) in adults.* American Psychological Association.

Bradley, R., Greene, J., Russ, E., Dutra, L., & Westen, D. (2005). A multidimensional meta-analysis of psychotherapy for PTSD. *American Journal of Psychiatry, 162*(2), 214–227.

Card, P. (2017). VA/DoD clinical practice guideline for the management of posttraumatic stress disorder and acute stress disorder. *Focus, 16*(4), 430–448.

Chapman, L., Morabito, D., Ladakakos, C., Schreier, H., & Knudson, M. M. (2001). The effectiveness of art therapy interventions in reducing posttraumatic stress disorder (PTSD) symptoms in traumatized adults. *Art Therapy, 18*(2), 100–104.

Cohen, J. A., Mannarino, A. P., & Deblinger, E. (2006). *Treating trauma and traumatic grief in children and adolescents.* Guilford Press.

Foa, E. B., Chrestman, K. R., & Gilboa-Schechtman, E. (2008). *Prolonged exposure therapy for adolescents with PTSD: Emotional processing of traumatic experiences: Therapist guide.* Oxford University Press.

Gendlin, E. T. (1978). *Focusing.* Everest House.

Henderson, P., Rosen, D., & Mascaro, N. (2007). Empirical study on the healing nature of mandalas. *Psychology of Aesthetics, Creativity, and the Arts, 1*(3), 148–154.

Herman, J. L. (1997). *Trauma and recovery: The aftermath of violence—from domestic abuse to political terror.* Basic Books.

Kapitan, L. (2018). *Introduction to art therapy research.* (2nd ed.) Routledge.

Klagsbrun, J., & Lennox, S. L. (2012). Clearing a space: An evidence-based approach for enhancing quality of life in women with breast cancer. *The Folio, 23*(1), 155–167.

McCann, I. L., & Pearlman, L. A. (1990). Vicarious traumatization: A framework for understanding the psychological effects of working with victims. *Journal of Traumatic Stress*, 3(1), 131–149.

Omaha, J. (2004). *Psychotherapeutic interventions for emotion regulation*. W. W. Norton.

Rappaport, L. (2009). *Focusing-riented art therapy*. Jessica Kingsley Publishers.

Resick, P. A., Monson, C. M., & Chard, K. M. (2016). *Cognitive processing therapy for PTSD: A comprehensive manual*. Guilford Press.

Roth, S., Newman, E., Pelcovitz, D., van der Kolk, B., & Mandel, F. S. (1997). Complex PTSD in victims exposed to sexual and physical abuse: Results from the *DSM-IV* field trial for posttraumatic stress disorder. *Journal of Traumatic Stress, 10*(4), 539–555. http://doi.org/10.1002/jts.2490100403.

Schouten, K. A., de Niet, G. J., Knipscheer, J. W., Kleber, R. J., & Hutschemaekers, G. J. M. (2015). The effectiveness of art therapy in treating traumatized adults: A systematic review on art therapy and trauma. *Trauma, Violence, and Abuse*, *16*(2), 220–228. doi:10.1177/1524838014555032

Schouten, K. A., van Hooren, S., Knipscheer, J. W., Kleber, R. J., & Hutschemaekers, G. J. M. (2019). Trauma-focused art therapy in the treatment of posttraumatic stress disorder: A pilot study. *Journal of Trauma & Dissociation*, *20*(1), 114–130.

Shapiro, F. (2007). EMDR and case conceptualization from an adaptive information processing perspective. In F. Shapiro, F. W. Kaslow, & L. Maxfield (Eds.), *Handbook of EMDR and family therapy processes* (pp. 3–34). John Wiley & Sons.

Talwar, S. (2007). Accessing traumatic memory through art making: An art therapy trauma protocol (ATTP). *The Arts in Psychotherapy*, *34*(1), 23–35.

van der Kolk, B. (2014). *The body keeps the score: Brain, mind, and body in the healing of trauma*. Penguin.

IMAGE CREDITS

Fig. 4.1: Generated using ChatGPT.

Fig. 4.2a: Generated using ChatGPT.

Fig. 4.2b: Generated using ChatGPT.

Fig. 4.2c: Generated using ChatGPT.

Fig. 4.3: Generated using ChatGPT.

Fig. 4.4: Generated using ChatGPT.

CHAPTER 5

Style, Color Palette, and Themes in Art Therapy

Insights into Emotional States and Trauma Processing

Post-traumatic stress disorder (PTSD) assessment typically involves interviews, questionnaires, and standardized tests. Standardized tests, such as the structured interview, Clinician-Administered PTSD Scale for *DSM-5* (CAPS-5) (Weathers, Blake et al., 2013), or PTSD Checklist for *DSM-5* (PCL-5) (Weathers, Litz et al., 2013), facilitate diagnosis and provide quantitative data about the client and their experience.

Many art therapists use art-based assessment instruments in addition to traditional measures, enriching the quantitative data gathered through those means with qualitative insights derived from engaging clients in the creative process (Jiménez et al., 2022). Art therapy facilitates access to feelings that clients may be unable to express verbally. This is particularly relevant in PTSD, where traumatic memories are often fragmented or suppressed.

This chapter presents the theoretical foundation of art as a means of assessment as well as its clinical utility and limitations. Upon completion of the chapter, readers will be able to:

1. Explain what is meant by the projective hypothesis.
2. Describe the elements of a client's artwork often used for assessing and monitoring progress.
3. Explain the limitations to the validity and reliability of employing art as an assessment tool.

Art Giving Voice and Form to Experience

Art has long been a means of expressing emotions, especially those that may be difficult to articulate verbally. In psychological practice, art and creative activities have gained traction as an effective method for assessing and addressing trauma and PTSD (Maddox et al., 2024). The belief that insight into a client's inner psyche can be acquired through creative activities is founded on the projective hypothesis.

The projective hypothesis refers to the notion that when confronted with ambiguous and unstructured stimuli—for example, a blank piece of paper, art materials, and instructions on how to draw how one is feeling—the responses elicited reflect the individual's unconscious needs, feelings, anxieties, motives, thoughts, conflicts, and prior behavioral conditioning (Basu, 2017). The assumption is that engagement with the creation of visual representation will help those with PTSD externalize and symbolically express complex or repressed emotions.

Therapists trained in art therapy will examine a client's artwork's style, color palette, and thematic elements. Focusing on these elements can provide the therapist insight into the client's emotional states and serve as a focal point for discussion and discovery.

The Role of Style in Emotional Expression

Therapists often focus on artistic style when using art and creative activities as part of an assessment process. Many believe clients' artistic styles mirror their emotional states and coping mechanisms.

Chaotic and Fragmented Styles. Artworks characterized by chaotic and fragmented elements often signify emotional overwhelm and disorganization. Jagged lines, irregular shapes, and disjointed compositions reflect a sense of internal chaos.

Research by Malchiodi (2012) emphasizes that fragmented, disjointed styles are frequently observed in individuals with PTSD. The hypothesis is that the fragmented nature of the artwork mirrors their fractured sense of self or intrusive memories.

Minimalist and Sparse Designs. Minimalist artwork, often sparse and monochromatic, can reflect emotional withdrawal or numbness. These characteristics suggest a state of emotional exhaustion or a coping mechanism rooted in avoidance.

Agnes Martin (1912–2004) was an American painter who had schizophrenia and other mental health issues throughout her life. She believed that she was hated as a child and that her mother's ruthless use of silence was a form of emotional abuse (Princenthal, 2015). Her paintings, sparse in design, represent her attempt at channeling the entirety of her focus onto the canvas so that other, more tempestuous feelings are kept at bay (Park, 2017). Samples of her work can be seen on the Museum of Modern Art's website at https://www.moma.org/artists/3787-agnes-martin.

Aggressive and Intense Mark-Making. Intense and aggressive artistic styles are frequently seen in individuals grappling with anger, frustration, or needing to release pent-up energy: bold, heavy strokes and saturated colors like red and black dominate such pieces. An illustrative example is Willem de Kooning's *Woman, I* (1950–52) (https://www.metmuseum.org/art/collection/search/687867). The painting employs dynamic, almost violent brushstrokes. It has been proposed that the creation reflects violence and a desire to attack the female form and was most likely linked to his traumatic childhood experience with an abusive mother (Taylor, 2022).

FIGURE 5.1 Edvard Munch's *The Scream* (1893)

Themes and Symbols

Art therapists are interested in the symbols employed in a client's creation. The themes, symbols, and imagery in clients' artwork often reflect the client's central concerns, fears, and coping strategies. Consider Edvard Munch's *The Scream* (1893), which is shown in Figure 5.1.

In the first viewing of the picture, one sees a figure standing on a bridge with its face elongated and contorted in agony. Behind the figure, however, is the backdrop of a turbulent sky and a swirling body of water. The images of swirling, chaotic background convey the artist's self-described existential crisis (Martinez, 2023).

Working with those challenged by PTSD, one often finds recurrent motifs and symbols such as images of entrapment or violence. These may indicate unresolved trauma. Eisenbach and associates (2015), for example, analyzed the art produced by 10 women between the ages of 24 and 60 who were victims of sexual trauma. The authors reported seven principal symbols that appeared more frequently in the artwork of sexual trauma victims. For example, most of the participants employ a symbol of their body in a fetal position. The authors hypothesized that the depiction symbolized the client's vulnerability and desire for safety and protection.

Art can also provide insight into the coping skills and healing that may be occurring. The introduction of protective symbols like shields or nurturing environments or themes of personal empowerment can signify adaptive coping mechanisms (Malchiodi, 2012). An excellent illustration of the healing and coping value of art can be found in the journey and art of Jane Orleman (1998). The artist was sexually molested from the age of 3 to 12 and experienced domestic violence until she was able to leave her family home at the age of 18. With the assistance of a therapist and her art, she was able to reclaim her strength, confidence, and resiliency. Her work *Dragging My Baggage into Paradise* suggests that while she will always have baggage, she is in control and not the baggage. As she noted, "It makes me smile to see the strength and confidence I show in managing that bag of woe" (Orleman, 2020).

While there is no singular way to interpret the symbols, their presentation within art therapy invites a dialogue between client and therapist to decode their meaning and facilitate the client's sharing of their experience, which they may struggle to articulate verbally (Morrell, 2011).

Color Palette as an Emotional Indicator

Color is pivotal in conveying mood and emotional states in art therapy. Colors can reflect emotional states and underlying trauma. Colors are often associated with specific emotions and moods, and these associations can vary across cultures and individuals. For instance, darker shades might indicate depressive symptoms (Hass-Cohen & Carr, 2008), with brighter and more varied colors felt to signify hope, joy, or emotional stability (PRO Expo Team, 2017).

Pablo Picasso (1881–1973) had his famous "blue period" from 1901 to 1904. During that time, he employed monochrome tones of blue, which was felt to reflect his sadness and low psychological state that was the result of the suicidal death of his friend, Carles Casagemas. An illustration of color reflecting mood can be found in his work *The Tragedy* (see Figure 5.2), a 1903 oil painting done in cool blues, which are felt to evoke his sadness and despair.

As is true for themes and symbols, a client's choice of color may reflect their expression and processing of emotions. Their choice of color and the theme they present can serve as a focal point for discussing their feelings and experiences (see Case Illustration 5.1).

FIGURE 5.2 *The Tragedy*

CASE ILLUSTRATION 5.1 **Color: Anger, Fear, and Guilt**

Rachael is a 29-year-old bartender who is the sole survivor of a traumatic car accident in which her father, mother, and younger brother died. Over the past three years, since the accident, she has experienced flashbacks and recurring nightmares. She reported feeling "emotionally numb, empty inside" and struggling to articulate her inner turmoil verbally.

During an art therapy session, Rachael was given various art materials and invited to create a painting. She selected bold red and black markers and used quick, forceful strokes to cover the canvas (see Figure 5.3).

FIGURE 5.3 Color: Anger, Fear, and Emptiness

The therapist hypothesized that using chaotic, forceful strokes of red and black reflected her internal conflicts. Additionally, the therapist believed that the choice of red, which is often associated with anger and fear, may very likely reflect her continued state of anxiety and heightened arousal. The inclusion of black was felt to speak to her emotional numbness and sense of hopelessness.

While the therapist working with Rachael (Illustration 5.1) drew hypotheses about the implications of her color choices and the use of chaotic lines and forceful strokes (see Figure 5.3), the drawing's value was that it facilitated discussions around the event and her feelings of survivor guilt and anger at not being able to save her family.

Evolution of Client Art and Trauma Processing

Changes in a client's artistic productions, whether in style, color palette, or themes, can reflect internal transformations, offering therapists a unique lens to evaluate therapeutic outcomes and guide intervention strategies (Malchiodi, 2012). Case Illustration 5.2 illustrates how changes in the client's art reflected changes in her grieving process. The transformation in her art provided a visual narrative of her healing.

CASE ILLUSTRATION 5.2 Moving from the Darkness of Grief

Agnes is a 72-year-old mother of 5. She came to therapy following the sudden, unexpected death of her husband of 52 years as a result of a ruptured aortic aneurysm. The incident occurred as the couple planned a trip to Barcelona, something they always had promised to do.

Agnes explained that since Albert's passing, she found it difficult to get out of bed, did not want to see any friends or family, and could not stop thinking about the "pained" expression on his face when the rupture occurred. She told the therapist: "When Albert passed, my soul went with him. I feel nothing. I just wish the Lord would take me."

The therapist employed cognitive behavioral therapy (CBT) as the primary mode of therapy and art activities as a vehicle to assist Agnes in conveying her feelings. During the initial session, Agnes was invited to use art materials to give form to how she was feeling. In her initial drawing, Agnes employed a monochromatic, black-and-white paint color scheme, reflecting her feelings of emptiness, finality, and a lack of vibrancy (see Figure 5.4a). This stark palette gave form to her deep sense of loss and grief.

Throughout the 16 weekly sessions, Agnes regained a sense of self (now as a single person) and a view of life that included re-engagement with her church, friends, and especially her family. While she continued to miss her husband, she began to re-experience a life of joy and love. Evidence of her progression is the dramatic expansion of her color palette to include vibrant colors in her final drawing (Figure 5.4b).

FIGURE 5.4A A Grieving Heart

FIGURE 5.4B Life and Love

In this case, the therapist felt that blending colors into the black-and-white base, rather than erasing it, suggested that Agnes integrated grief into a broader life context. Agnes's re-engagement with family and friends supported this hypothesis.

A Question of Validity

The validity and reliability of art as an assessment tool have been and continue to be challenged. Critics argue that subjective interpretations undermine the scientific credibility of art as an assessment tool (Betts, 2006; Lilienfeld et al., 2000). In response, standardized art-based assessment tools have been developed. Assessment tools, such as the Silver Drawing Test (Silver, 2007) and the Diagnostic Drawing Series (DDS) (Cohen, 1986/1994/2012; Cohen & Mills, 2016), are structured employing specific prompts, materials, and scoring systems to ensure consistency and reliability across diverse populations.

Despite its utility, art as an assessment tool has limitations. Subjective interpretation of artistic expressions challenges validity and reliability, and much more research is needed to validate its utility.

It appears that the most effective approach to the assessment of PTSD and trauma-related disorders is to incorporate objective measures such as standardized evaluation procedures (formal assessments, behavioral checklists, portfolio evaluation) and subjective approaches such as interpreting the client's artwork (Betts, 2006). This combination provides therapists with qualitative and quantitative data for comprehensive diagnostic insights.

From Knowledge to Application

Having read about the value of attending to a client's artistic style, thematic elements, and color palette to gain insight into a client's emotional state, you are invited to apply what you have learned. Exercise 5.1 presents you with Vincent van Gogh's *The Starry Night* (1889). Use your best clinical insights and knowledge of art as a projective technique to interpret the artist's mental and emotional state.

EXERCISE 5.1 ***The Starry Night***

Directions: To counterbalance your subjectivity and bias, you may find it helpful to engage with this exercise with a colleague or classmate.

Part 1: Take time to observe, in close detail, van Gogh's *The Starry Night* (Figure 5.5).

FIGURE 5.5 *The Starry Night*

Now with your clinical hat on, hypothesize about the emotions and potential psychological struggles the artist is experiencing. Write your interpretations below.

Style (e.g., intensity and movement of brush strokes)

____

____

Symbols and Themes (e.g., sky, moon, cypress tree)

____

____

Color Palette (e.g., blues and vibrant yellows)

____

____

____

Part II: Review the following information as it validates or conflicts with your hypotheses and interpretation. If needed, adjust your initial interpretations (Part I).

Vincent van Gogh's *The Starry Night* was created during his stay at the Saint-Paul-de-Mausole asylum. According to Nolen and associates (2020), van Gogh most likely suffered from comorbid illnesses. It appeared that since young adulthood, he experienced bipolar mood disorder in combination with (traits of) a borderline personality disorder as underlying vulnerability. He experienced at least two episodes of delirium and a depressive episode with psychotic features. On July 27, 1890, in a field near Auvers, Vincent shot himself in the chest with a revolver.

Part III: Many have offered their opinion about the meaning of this work. Compare your interpretations to those offered by Mavrouis (2024), Artble (n.d.), Qi (2024).

Style

- Swirling sky reflecting artist's internal turmoil
- A blend of swirling, chaotic skies and tranquil landscapes, mirroring his oscillation between emotional turmoil and moments of clarity

Composition and Brush Strokes

- Violent energy in the sky, as opposed to the calm of the village, is symbolic of his bipolar experience
- Brightening light in the night sky speaks of the journey into energizing hypomania and the bright high of mania
- Dark silhouettes and cypress (a symbol of death) reflect the artist's depression

Colors

- Dominance of blue reflecting melancholy
- Yellow as a sense of hope
- The interplay of dark blues and vibrant yellows symbolizes an oscillation between despair and hope.

The Takeaway

Projective theory and its applications in art therapy are valuable tools for psychological assessment and therapeutic intervention. Clinicians can use a client's art production to bridge gaps where traditional assessment methods may fall short.

Integrating art-based methods with other evidence-based approaches holds promise for advancing trauma-informed care. Working with clients' art can facilitate access to implicit memories, foster emotional expression, and engage clients in discussion around topics previously too complex to discuss. Future research should focus on integrating qualitative insights with quantitative validation to solidify the role of projective techniques in art therapy.

Keystones

- PTSD assessment typically involves standardized tools such as CAPS-5 and PCL-5, providing quantitative data.
- Art-based assessments, reflecting the projective hypothesis, can enrich these measures by offering qualitative insights into emotional states and trauma, complementing verbal expression.
- Art therapy helps clients externalize repressed emotions and express fragmented traumatic memories.
- Style, color palette, and thematic elements are focal points for understanding a client's inner world.
- The evolution of a client's artwork can provide a nonverbal narrative of therapeutic progress, reflecting emotional progress and healing.
- The validity of employing art as an assessment tool is challenged by its subjectivity.
- Combining quantitative measures (e.g., CAPS-5, PCL-5) with qualitative art-based methods ensures a comprehensive understanding of trauma.

ADDITIONAL RESOURCES

Adams, L. S. (1993). *Art and psychoanalysis*. Routledge.

Cohen, B. M., Barnes, M.-M., & Rankin, A. B. (1995). *Managing traumatic stress through art: Drawing from the center*. Sidran Press.

De Masi, L. (2024). *Understanding colour psychology: The psychological effects of colours on emotions, moods, and perceptions*. Louise De Masi Watercolour Art. https://www.louisedemasi.com/insights/2024/6/18/understanding-colour-psychology?srsltid=AfmBOorucA-Hpz6sgAhBcl8HM_QgDFK8FTv4DehdYZXbEanKa7NBCamY

REFERENCES

Artble. (n.d.). *Starry Night analysis*. Artble. https://www.artble.com/artists/vincent_van_gogh/paintings/starry_night/more_information/analysis

Basu, J. (2017). Projective hypothesis. In V. Zeigler-Hill & T. Shackelford. (Eds.). *Encyclopedia of personality and individual differences*. Springer. https://doi.org/10.1007/978-3-319-28099-8_64-1

Betts, D. J. (2006). Art therapy assessments and rating instruments: Do they measure up? *The Arts in Psychotherapy, 33*(5), 422–434. https://doi.org/10.1016/j.aip.2006.08.001

Cohen, B. M. (1986/1994/2012). *The Diagnostic Drawing Series rating guide*. Unpublished guidebook. (All documents available from Barry M. Cohen via landmarc@cox.net (preferred) or PO Box 9853, Alexandria, VA, USA 22304.)

Cohen, B. M., & Mills, A. (2016). The Diagnostic Drawing Series (DDS) at thirty: Art therapy assessment and research. In D. E. Gussak & M. L. Rosal (Eds.), *The Wiley handbook of art therapy* (pp. 558–568). Wiley Blackwell.

Eisenbach, N., Snir, S., & Regev, D. (2015). Identification and characterization of symbols emanating from the spontaneous artwork of survivors of childhood trauma. *The Arts in Psychotherapy, 44*, 45–56.

Hass-Cohen, N., & Carr, R. (2008). *Art therapy and clinical neuroscience*. Jessica Kingsley Publishers.

Jiménez, C. P., Peral, J., & Webler, M. (2022). Observation-based assessment in art therapy (OBAS-ATT): A process-oriented instrument combining qualitative and quantitative data. *Art Therapy*, 39(4), 168–180. https://doi.org/10.1080/17454832.2021.1998164

Lilienfeld, S. O., Wood, J. M., & Garb, H. N. (2000). The scientific status of projective techniques. *Psychological Science in the Public Interest, 1*(2), 27–66. https://doi.org/10.1111/1529-1006.002

Maddox, G. A., Bodner, G. E., Christian, M. W., & Williamson, P. (2024). On the effectiveness of visual arts therapy for traumatic experiences: A systematic review and meta-analysis. *Clinical Psychology & Psychotherapy, 31*(4), e3041. https://doi.org/10.1002/cpp.3041

Malchiodi, C. A. (2012). *Handbook of art therapy* (2nd ed.). Guilford Press.

Martinez, I. (2023). *The analysis of Munch's "The Scream."* 1st Art Gallery. https://www.1st-art-gallery.com/article/the-analysis-of-munchs-the-scream/?srsltid=AfmBOoqv_yKNlma57UuUgOKMxF-tE8md5h5d1fIxMmTvnVwoWJcLk0JN

Mavrouis, I. (2024). *The Starry Night*. MyNeuroNews. https://myneuronews.com/2024/09/21/the-starry-night/.

Morrell, M. (2011). Signs and symbols: Art and language in art therapy. *Journal of Clinical Art Therapy, 1*(1), 25–32. https://digitalcommons.lmu.edu/jcat/vol1/iss1/

Nolen, W. A., van Meekeren, E., Voskuil, P., & van Tilburg, W. (2020). New vision on the mental problems of Vincent van Gogh; results from a bottom-up approach using (semi-)structured diagnostic interviews. *International Journal of Bipolar Disorders, 8*, 30. https://journalbipolardisorders.springeropen.com/articles/10.1186/s40345-020-00196-z#citeas

Orleman, J. (1998). *Telling secrets: An artist's journey through childhood trauma*. Child Welfare League of America.

Orleman, J. (2020). Dragging my baggage into paradise by Jane Orleman. Artist Trust. https://artisttrust.org/dragging-my-baggage-into-paradise-by-jane-orleman/

Park, R. (2017). *Agnes Martin: Strength and vulnerability through minimalism*. Art UK. https://artuk.org/discover/stories/agnes-martin-strength-and-vulnerability-through-minimalism

Princenthal, N. (2015). *Agnes Martin: Her life and art*. Thames & Hudson.

Pro Expo Team (2017). *Color psychology—the meaning of colors and their traits*. Pro Expo. https://tradeshowbestpractices.com/2017/08/03/color-psychology-meaning-colors-traits/

Qi, F. (2024). *The symbolic use of color in Vincent van Gogh's The Starry Night*. Francis Academic Press. https://francis-press.com/uploads/papers/7P1UzmI5OTjd9NNZJYqLjZbmzy77nABdjPm6gsvC.pd

Silver, R. A. (2007). *The Silver drawing test and draw a story: Assessing depression, aggression, and cognitive skills*. Routledge.

Taylor, G. J. (2022). *Willem de Kooning's women: A psychoanalytic exploration*. International Psychoanalytic Books.

Weathers, F. W., Blake, D. D., Schnurr, P. P., Kaloupek, D. G., Marx, B. P., & Keane, T. M. (2013). *The clinician-administered PTSD scale for* DSM-5 *(CAPS-5)*. [Assessment] U.S. Department of Veterans Affairs. https://www.ptsd.va.gov/professional/assessment/adult-int/caps.asp. Scale available from the National Center for PTSD at www.ptsd.va.gov.

Weathers, F. W., Litz, B. T., Keane, T. M., Palmieri, P. A., Marx, B. P., & Schnurr, P. P. (2013). *The PTSD checklist for* DSM-5 *(PCL-5)*. U.S. Department of Veterans Affairs. https://www.ptsd.va.gov/professional/assessment/adult-sr/ptsd-checklist.asp. Scale available from the National Center for PTSD at www.ptsd.va.gov.

IMAGE CREDITS

Fig. 5.1: Edvard Munch, "The Scream," https://commons.wikimedia.org/wiki/File:The_Scream_by_Edvard_Munch,_1893_-_Nasjonalgalleriet.png, 1893.

Fig. 5.2: Pablo Picasso, "The Tragedy," https://www.wikiart.org/en/pablo-picasso/the-tragedy-1903, 1903.

Fig. 5.3: Generated using ChatGPT.

Fig. 5.4a: Generated using ChatGPT.

Fig. 5.4b: Generated using ChatGPT.

Fig. 5.5: Vincent Van Gogh, "Starry Night," https://commons.wikimedia.org/wiki/File:Van_Gogh_-_Starry_Night_-_Google_Art_Project.jpg, 1889.

PART III

Special Populations

CHAPTER 6

Children and Adolescents Experiencing Trauma and PTSD

While post-traumatic stress disorder (PTSD) is often associated with adults, children and adolescents can also develop this disorder. More than two-thirds of children have experienced trauma as a result of abuse, neglect, assault, exploitation, violence witnessed with the family or community, natural disasters, or the sudden loss of a loved one by the age of 16 years (Lawrence-Sidebottom et al., 2024). Being at critical points of their development, the experience of trauma can have profound effects on a child's or teen's neurological development and their emotional, cognitive, and social functioning.

Given the potential damage trauma can create, early intervention is vital. One significant challenge, however, is that traditional evidence-based therapeutic modalities often struggle to address the complexities of trauma in younger populations, as verbal expression may be limited by developmental or psychological factors (Malchiodi, 2020).

Art therapy is a powerful modality for addressing trauma in children and youth, enabling them to access, express, and process traumatic experiences in creative and nonverbal ways. The current chapter explores the use of art therapy with children and adolescents experiencing trauma and PTSD, providing a theoretical foundation, empirical evidence, and practical guidelines for implementation.

Upon completion of this chapter, readers will be able to:

1. Describe the impact that trauma can have on children and adolescents;
2. Explain the unique value of art as a therapeutic modality of assisting children and adolescents struggling with the effects of trauma, and;
3. Outline a generic model or approach to employ art therapy with children and adolescents.

Trauma and PTSD in Children and Adolescents

Children and adolescents bring a unique vulnerability to traumatic events. Adverse childhood experiences (ACEs) are potentially traumatic events that occur in childhood (0–17 years). These can include experiencing violence, abuse, neglect, or witnessing violence (Centers for Disease Control and Prevention, 2019). They also include aspects of the child's environment that can undermine their sense of safety, stability, and bonding (Felitti et al., 1998). It is believed that more than two-thirds of all children have encountered at least one adverse childhood experience by the age of 16 (SAMHSA, 2023). While these data are alarming, they are likely underestimates of the actual number of children and youth impacted by crisis and trauma (Owens & Parsons, 2025). The very secretive and stigmatizing nature of some types of traumatic events (e.g., physical and sexual abuse) can lead to the underreporting of prevalence and incidence (Saunders & Adams, 2014).

Exposure to ACEs and traumatic events can have both immediate and long-standing negative impacts on a child or teen's social-emotional-behavioral development, academic achievement, mental health, and even brain development (Maynard et al., 2019). Children and adolescents struggling with the impact of trauma may exhibit developmental regression, somatic complaints, and difficulties in school or social settings (Alameddine, 2025). Additional symptoms can include hyperarousal, avoidance, intrusive thoughts, nightmares, emotional numbing, and emotional dysregulation (American Psychiatric Association, 2013). For children and teens, trauma can have a significant impact on their neurological, behavioral, and emotional functioning (Maynard et al., 2019).

Given the extent and potential long-term effects of trauma on a child or teen, early identification and intervention are crucial. A challenge when treating children and adolescents with trauma is that they are less likely to express their traumatic experiences verbally. This reluctance to disclose and discuss their experiences can limit the effectiveness of more traditional talk therapies (Cohen & Mannarino, 2004). Art therapy provides a dynamic and effective means for helping children and adolescents navigate the effects of trauma.

The Value of Art as a Medium of Therapy for Children and Adolescents

Young children and teens often lack the verbal skills needed to process and express complex emotions and inner turmoil associated with trauma. Art provides an alternative through which they can convey their feelings and the turmoil being experienced.

Art—through drawing, painting, or other creative forms—engages the brain's cognitive and emotional centers, helping young individuals regulate emotions and gain insight into their experiences (Malchiodi, 2020). The nonverbal nature of art allows them to process difficult memories and emotions without being retraumatized by the demands of verbal recounting (Hinz, 2019). The art produced can then be a focal point to facilitate a therapeutic exchange with their therapist (Rubin, 2016).

In addition to serving as a means of expression, the nature of the material employed and the task assigned can have therapeutic value. For example, clay and sculpture provide unique opportunities for somatic expression, which is especially beneficial for children and adolescents who may not yet have the words to articulate their emotions or feelings of psychological distress. For a client, working clay allows the tactile experience to connect physical sensations with emotional expression, helping them process emotions stored in the body (Elbrecht, 2019). This technique can be beneficial for addressing trauma, anger, and grief, as manipulating clay offers a release for the pent-up energy associated with these emotions (see Case Illustration 6.1).

CASE ILLUSTRATION 6.1 Elijah: The Magic of Clay

While now living with his mother in a safe environment, eight-year-old Elijah experienced eight years of exposure to chronic domestic abuse and violence. He was referred to therapy by his mother due to his significant difficulty regulating his emotions, particularly in response to perceived threats or stressors. According to his mother, Elijah experienced episodes of explosive anger, hypervigilance, and difficulty engaging in peer relationships.

Initially Elijah was resistant to talk with the therapist about his experiences or even his current feelings. Regardless of the topic or the nature of the therapist's query, Elijah would remain quiet. The therapist acknowledged how difficult it could be to talk to someone new. She also noted that she found it easier when she could relax. With that as a backdrop, the therapist provided Elijah with a block of clay and invited him to feel it—touch it—squeeze it.

While hesitant at first, Elijah picked up the clay and rapidly transitioned from touching it to pounding and twisting the material. The therapist was supportive and after a few minutes gently invited him to notice how it felt to squeeze the clay and then let go.

As he repeated this pattern of squeezing and releasing, the therapist suggested that he breathe in rhythm with the squeeze, let-go, pattern. These two physical interventions helped Elijah to experience a reduction in tension and continuing the manipulation of the clay, he began to share his story.

The materials and the "project" employed can be selected for targeted therapeutic goals. For example, mandalas (see Figure 6.1) are circular designs that offer a sense of balance and focus, making them a valuable tool for young clients experiencing anxiety (Støre & Jakobsson, 2022). They are often employed in the beginning of a session to help the client calm and focus.

FIGURE 6.1 Mandala Pyramide

The repetitive nature of mandala-making grounds the child and reduces feelings of overwhelm. Studies show that children who engage in mandala art report decreased anxiety and improved ability to regulate emotions (Singh et al., 2023).

Another task, that of **creating collages and employment of mixed media, are powerful tools for facilitating narrative construction.** These techniques involve cutting, assembling, and reassembling materials such as photographs, magazine images, fabric, and other found objects. The client would select images, words, phrases, pictures, or colors from the magazines and newspapers and compile a reflection of how they are feeling, or what they desire, or a visual presentation of their life stories. These materials can help young clients integrate disparate experiences into a coherent narrative. The process allows a youthful client to create a visual narrative that reflects their experiences, struggles, or aspirations (Woollett et al., 2020). The creation of a collage and the moving of materials to arrange and rearrange the creation allows the younger client to reframe negative experiences or feelings and gain a sense of agency and control over their emotions and experiences (McClymont, 2023). This was certainly the case for Alisson, a 13-year-old who narrowly escaped a house fire and struggled for 9 months with intrusive images of fire, house damage, and her tears and fear. In her fourth therapy session, she created a collage that de-emphasized the fire and fear and highlighted her strengths and a hopeful, brighter future (see Figure 6.2).

FIGURE 6.2 Stronger, Brighter Future

Research supports the efficacy of art therapy for reducing PTSD symptoms and improving emotional well-being in children and adolescents. Meta-analysis (see Morison et al., 2022) found that creative arts therapies, including art therapy, significantly reduced trauma-related symptoms compared to control groups.

Designing Art Therapy Interventions

Once again, it must be stated that there is no single formula, template, or approach to be used when employing art therapy with children and teens experiencing the effects of trauma. Each child and adolescent may respond differently to materials and methods.

Therapists need to engage in a comprehensive assessment of client-based developmental readiness, trauma history, and temperament so they can tailor their approach to the uniqueness of each client. While several markers should guide one's employment of art therapy with children and adolescents experiencing trauma or PTSD, flexibility is essential.

Preparation

As is true of all effective therapy, building a trusting relationship and working alliance is essential to the effectiveness of art therapy. This is especially true when children and adolescents are the victims of trauma and are likely struggling with trust and emotional safety issues.

Therapists working with these clients must prioritize creating a secure space where the clients feel comfortable and safe expressing themselves. The therapist must exhibit empathy, consistency, and predictability in the therapeutic environment.

The space should be welcoming and calm. Age-appropriate, non-threatening, or re-traumatizing diverse art materials, such as paper, crayons, markers, clay, paint, and collage supplies, should be provided.

Selecting Developmentally Appropriate Materials and Techniques

Working with children requires a nuanced understanding of their developmental stages to ensure that interventions align with their cognitive, emotional, and motor abilities. The selection of both materials and "tasks" should be done with a sensitivity toward clients' cognitive, psycho-emotional, and social level of development. For example, with an understanding of Piagetian theory of cognitive development (Malik & Marwaha, 2023), a therapist employing art therapy with children in the preoperational stage (ages 2–7) may prefer tactile and sensory-rich materials. Therapists working with this population might consider using simple, tactile materials like crayons, finger paints, or modeling clay (Rubin, 2016). Adolescents, on the other hand, may gravitate towards expressive and symbolic media. Given their cognitive abilities to handle more abstract concepts and their immersion in digital technology, adolescents may prefer engaging with digital art and technology to share feelings and disclose concerns via picture or video rather than via free drawing (Zeevi, 2021).

While the materials employed should be sensitive to the developmental level of the client, tasks, when assigned, should also consider the client's level of development and the therapeutic goals. For example, while perhaps employing nonthreatening unstructured materials and tasks in the early sessions as a way of encouraging spontaneity and creativity, therapists may introduce resistive materials such as a clay for clients experiencing issues with emotional regulation, fluid materials such as finger paints and watercolors to facilitate relaxation and emotional expression or even structured tasks and materials such as collages to provide safety and a sense of containment for clients overwhelmed or anxious (Haiblum-Itskovitch et al., 2018).

Structuring the Session

While each session needs to be responsive to the needs of the client and the issues needing to be addressed at that time, several elements should be considered when employing art therapy with children and adolescents impacted by trauma.

Opening Ritual/Grounding Activity: Establishing rituals, such as beginning each session with a calming activity, perhaps coloring of a mandala, helps create a sense of stability (Pifalo, 2007). Sessions can start with a breathing exercise or a simple art task (e.g., coloring). Sensory art materials (e.g., clay and textured paper) may help engage the client in a tactile, soothing experience.

Session Tasks: It is important to explain each task's purpose clearly. With children and teens struggling with the effects of trauma, the tasks should be graded, starting with nonthreatening activities and gradually introducing movement toward depictions of the experience.

Trauma Narrative Reconstruction: The therapist gradually guides the client in depicting their trauma story using art (Campbell et al., 2016). This could involve sequential drawings to narrate events or the creation of collages that represent "before," "during," and "after" the trauma.

Emphasis will be placed on ensuring the client experiences control and choice, allowing the client to modify or reconstruct the story to reflect resilience and empowerment. With the focus on reconstructing the child's narrative, the therapist will direct them to create projects with positive self-identity and future aspirations, such as creating a "shield of strengths," a "Superhero character," or some other form representing their resilience (Kim, 2018). The goal is to help the traumatized child or teen to feel empowered and in control of their experiences.

Reflection: The art production offers a concrete presentation of the client's internalized feelings, providing both a focal point for reflection and discussion and a visual record for further discussion (Keane, 2017). The therapist may use prompts such as "What does this part of your drawing mean to you?" or "How did it feel to create this?" to encourage the youth to share their thoughts about their creation, either verbally or by adding written elements to their artwork. Rather than the therapist's analysis, the focus is on the youth's interpretations and emotions.

Closing Positive Ritual: As is true for all modalities of therapy, in ending an art therapy session it is helpful to close with a summary of the activities and progress made within the session, encourage the client to share their thoughts and concerns, address homework or between-sessions activities that are prescribed, invite lingering questions, and end on a positive note. With art therapy with younger clients, it is helpful to use a consistent activity that provides closure. For example, a child or teen may be asked to draw their symbol of hope or write a word or phrase such as "strong" or "empowered" to positively end the session with the client feeling grounded.

Case Illustration 6.2 highlights the use of these elements in the treatment of a 12-year-old girl traumatized by years of parental emotional and physical abuse.

CASE ILLUSTRATION 6.2 Jazmine

Jazmine is a 12-year-old girl referred to art therapy due to trauma stemming from a year of emotional and physical abuse by her new stepfather. Recently placed in foster care, she struggles with trust, emotional regulation, and a sense of safety. She exhibits depression, anxiety, withdrawal, and difficulty articulating her feelings. The following provides a condensed view of the elements employed in her therapy.

Preparation

The therapy room is designed with calm, soothing colors and contains various art materials, including paper, markers, paints, clay, and collage supplies. At the start of each session, Jazmine is given time to familiarize herself with the space and materials and to engage with the therapist. The therapist uses a warm, nonjudgmental demeanor, allowing Jazmine to approach art-making at her own pace.

A clear structure and somewhat routine pattern structure each session to reduce anxiety, ensuring Jazmine knows what to expect.

1. **Opening Ritual/Grounding Activity**

   Each session begins with a grounding activity. Jazmine shared her desire and liking to color mandalas as an initial activity. This provided time for the therapist to check in on Jazmine's current condition before proceeding to a session task.

2. **Task Directions**

   The specific tasks for each session were developed to reintroduce Jazmine to her trauma narrative slowly. While presented with a task, the therapist allowed Jazmine to create art about her experiences at her own pace, with opportunities to modify or reinterpret them. For example, during the initial sessions, the tasks were open-ended, inviting her to develop something that reflected her feelings or what would represent a safe space. In the third session, she was invited to create a "feelings mask," where Jazmine decorated one side to show how she felt on the outside and the other to represent her inner emotions. In the later sessions, Jazmine was guided in constructing a "Timeline of My Strengths," using sequential drawings to depict moments of resilience.

3. **Trauma Narrative Reconstruction**

   In later sessions, Jazmine created a series of collages representing "Before, During, and After" the trauma (see Figure 6.3).

   FIGURE 6.3 Jazmine: From Happy to Sad to Withdrawn

   The illustration allowed the therapist to help Jazmine discuss the horror of the experience of being abused as well as her current feelings of extreme sadness and a sense that she is all alone. The collage also provided the invitation to discuss how happy and social she was prior to the experience of the abuse and use that as a goal for therapy.

4. **Reflection**

   At the end of each session, the therapist and Jazmine reviewed her artwork and reflected on its meaning. The therapist used prompts like "What do you see when you look at this?" and "How did it feel to make this part?" This discussion empowered Jazmine to articulate her emotions and recognize her growth.

5. **Closing Positive Ritual**

   The sessions would always end on a positive note. In the later sessions, Jazmine would create a drawing or symbol of hope, empowerment, and safety. On several occasions, she labeled the drawing with a positive word or phrase about herself. "I am strong and creative" is one such phrase that she placed on a keepsake tile. The therapist would have her take these with her to remind her of her strengths and resilience.

Outcome

Through art therapy, Jazmine began to rebuild trust, process her trauma, and foster resilience. She became more comfortable expressing her feelings, both through art and verbally. Her foster parents reported seeing her as more relaxed and socially engaged. Jazmine described feeling calmer, more in control, stronger, and re-engaging with her peers at school.

Integrating Art Therapy with Other Evidence-Based Modalities

Art therapy is a versatile, adaptable therapeutic that is particularly effective when integrated with other evidence-based therapeutic modalities, such as cognitive-behavioral and narrative therapy.

Combining art therapy with trauma-focused cognitive-behavioral therapy (TF-CBT) can use art to explore and process traumatic memories and identify and challenge maladaptive thoughts and behaviors. Trauma-focused cognitive behavioral art therapy (Heijman et al., 2024) incorporates TF-CBT's core components, such as psychoeducation, gradual exposure, and cognitive restructuring, within an art-based framework.

Children engaged with TF-CBAT may create a timeline of their trauma history through drawings. This activity would enable them to process their experiences visually and at their own pace (Cohen et al., 2017), reducing the risk of retraumatization. In the process, children and adolescents are encouraged to revisit their traumatic history and create artwork representing their strengths, coping skills, and aspirations for the future. This positive focus helps reframe the trauma narrative, fostering a sense of empowerment and hope (Malchiodi, 2020). A recent study by Heijman and associates (Heijman et al., 2024) demonstrated the effectiveness of trauma-focused art therapy in reducing PTSD symptoms in adolescents, particularly when combined with psychoeducation and relaxation techniques.

Narrative therapy is another approach that has integrated art as a therapeutic modality (Madigan, 2011). Narrative therapy encourages clients to reauthor their life stories, emphasizing their strengths and resilience (Baştemur & Baş, 2021). Narrative art therapy builds on this concept by incorporating visual storytelling (Van Lith et al., 2018). Children and adolescents create sequential art pieces or "storyboards" to externalize their experiences, allowing for cognitive restructuring and emotional catharsis. Kalthom and associates (2024) found that self-narrative art therapy significantly reduced PTSD symptoms among Syrian war-affected children aged 6 to 12.

Integrating art therapy with evidence-based modalities is an effective way to assist young clients express difficult emotions and engage in cognitive restructuring and recovery from trauma (Woollett et al., 2020).

From Knowledge to Application

As presented in this chapter, employing art therapy with children and adolescents requires a nuanced understanding of their developmental stages to ensure that interventions align with their cognitive, emotional, and motor abilities. The intervention also needs to be responsive to the client's unique experience with trauma. Exercise 6.1 invites you to develop a therapeutic approach for three unique clients.

EXERCISE 6.1 Decisions to be Made

Directions: Part I provides some basic case information on three clients. Using this information, respond in Part II to the therapy decisions you need to make if engaged with these clients. Doing this exercise with a classmate or colleague may be valuable.

Part I: Client information

Case Information	Max	Louise	Rebecca
Age	8 years old	5 years old	16 years old
Traumatic experience	Experienced his stepfather beating his mother	Barely escaped a house fire	Was attacked and sexually assaulted by her neighbor
Symptoms	Unregulated emotions, aggression, and self-harm	Fearful of going to sleep, has night terrors, doesn't want to leave her mother at home alone, and refuses to go to school	Extremely withdrawn, stays in her room, refuses to wear anything but oversized clothing

Part II: Decisions to be Made

Complete the following table identifying your response to the various decisions that would need to be made in treating each client with art therapy.

Task	Max	Louise	Rebecca
For the initial session what medium or art supplies would you employ? Why?			
What opening ritual or grounding activity might you use for each session?			
In considering tasks to be used in sessions, how would you gradually guide each client to trauma narrative reconstruction?			
What closing ritual would you employ to assist the client to feel grounded and positive following a session?			

The Takeaway

Art therapy serves as a valuable tool in assisting children and adolescents to navigate the complexities of trauma and PTSD. Art therapy provides a strategy to bypass verbal limitations, foster self-expression, and promote healing.

Art therapists can tailor interventions to meet their young clients' unique developmental, emotional, and social needs by employing various techniques, such as collage, clay, and mandalas. Research supports the effectiveness of art therapy, especially when used in conjunction with evidence-based interventions such as trauma-informed cognitive therapy or narrative therapy.

Keystones

- More than two-thirds of children experience trauma from abuse, neglect, violence, or disasters by age 16.
- Trauma profoundly affects neurological, emotional, cognitive, and social development in children and adolescents.
- Verbal expression may be limited in younger populations, making traditional talk therapies less effective.
- Art therapy enables children to externalize and process trauma creatively without the retraumatization of verbal recounting.
- Effective sessions include grounding activities, trauma narrative reconstruction, therapeutic reflection, and positive closure.
- Meta-analyses and studies confirm that art therapy reduces PTSD symptoms and improves emotional well-being in children and adolescents.

ADDITIONAL RESOURCES

Berberian, M. & Davis, B. (Eds.) (2020). *Art therapy practices for resilient youth: A strengths-based approach to at-promise children and adolescents.* Routledge.

Malchiodi, C. (2021). *Creative interventions with traumatized children* (2nd ed.). Guilford Press.

Regev, D. (2023). Special issue: Arts therapies with children and adolescents—editorial. *Children, 10*(1), 110. https://doi.org/10.3390/children10010110

REFERENCES

Alameddine A. (2025). Developmental regression associated with PTSD in children: a poorly defined and understudied phenomenon. *Scandinavian Journal of Child and Adolescent Psychiatry and Psychology, 13*(1), 54–56. https://doi.org/10.2478/sjcapp-2025-0006

American Psychiatric Association. (2013). *Diagnostic and statistical manual of mental disorders* (5th ed.). American Psychiatric Association. https://doi.org/10.1176/appi.books.9780890425596

Baştemur, Ş., & Baş, E. (2021). Integration of narrative therapy with expressive art practices. [Öyküsel terapinin dışavurumcu sanat uygulamaları ile bütünleşmesi]. *Psikiyatride Güncel Yaklaşimlar, 13*(1), 146–169. doi: https://doi.org/10.18863/pgy.771319

Campbell, M., Decker, K. P., Kruk, K., & Deaver, S. P. (2016). Art therapy and cognitive processing therapy for combat-related PTSD: A randomized controlled trial. *Art Therapy, 33*(4), 169–177. https://doi.org/10.1080/07421656.2016.1226643

Centers for Disease Control and Prevention (2019). *Adverse childhood experiences (ACEs) prevention resource for action: A compilation of the best available evidence.* National Center for Injury Prevention and Control, Centers for Disease Control and Prevention.

Cohen, J. A., & Mannarino, A. P. (2004). Treatment of childhood traumatic grief. *Journal of Clinical Child and Adolescent Psychology: the Official Journal for the Society of Clinical Child and Adolescent Psychology, American Psychological Association, Division 53, 33*(4), 819–831. https://doi.org/10.1207/s15374424jccp3304_17

Cohen, J. A., Mannarino, A. P., & Deblinger, E. (2017). *Treating trauma and traumatic grief in children and adolescents* (2nd ed.). Guilford Press.

Cohen-Yatziv, L., & Regev, D. (2019). The effectiveness and contribution of art therapy work with children in 2018—what progress has been made so far? A systematic review. *International Journal of Art Therapy, 24*(3), 100–112.

Elbrecht, C. (2019). *Clay field therapy as a sensorimotor art therapy.* https://www.sensorimotorarttherapy.com/blog/clay-field-therapy-as-a-sensorimotor-art-therapy

Felitti, V. J., Anda, R. F., Nordenberg, D., Williamson, D. F., Spitz, A. M., Edwards, V., Koss, M. P., & Marks, J. S. (1998). Relationship of childhood abuse and household dysfunction to many of the leading causes of death in adults: The Adverse Childhood Experiences (ACE) Study. *American Journal of Preventive Medicine, 14*(4), 245–258.

Haiblum-Itskovitch, S., Czamanski-Cohen, J., & Galili, G. (2018). Emotional response and changes in heart rate variability following art-making with three different art materials. *Frontiers in Psychology, 9*, 968. https://doi.org/10.3389/fpsyg.2018.00968

Heijman, J., Wouters, H., Schouten, K. A., & Haeyen, S. (2024). Effectiveness of trauma-focused art therapy (TFAT) for psychological trauma: Study protocol of a multiple-baseline single-case experimental design. *BMJ Open, 14*(1), e081917. https://doi.org/10.1136/bmjopen-2023-081917

Hinz, L. D. (2019). *Expressive therapies continuum: A framework for using art in therapy* (2nd ed.). Routledge.

Kalthom, M., Nazeri, A. & Faramarzi, S. (2024). The effectiveness of self-narrative art therapy in reducing (PTSD) symptoms among war-affected Syrian children. *Journal of Child and Adolescent Trauma, 18*, 209–216. https://doi.org/10.1007/s40653-024-00683-w

Keane, C. (2017). *An expert on school-based art therapy explains how art therapy helps children make sense of the insensible.* American Art Therapy Association. https://arttherapy.org/art-therapy-helps-children-make-sense-of-the-insensible/

Kim, E. (2018). Art therapy with homeless children: Role of art therapy on complex trauma event. *Expressive Therapies Capstone Theses, 96*. https://digitalcommons.lesley.edu/cgi/viewcontent.cgi?article=1093&context=expressive_theses

Lawrence-Sidebottom, D., Huffman, L. G., Beam, A. B., Guerra, R., Parikh, A., Roots, M., & Huberty, J. (2024). Rates of trauma exposure and posttraumatic stress in a pediatric digital mental health intervention: Retrospective analysis of associations with anxiety and depressive symptom improvement over time. *JMIR Pediatrics and Parenting, 7*, e5560. https://pediatrics.jmir.org/2024/1/e55560

Madigan, S. (2011). *Narrative therapy.* American Psychological Association.

Malchiodi, C. A. (2020). *Trauma and expressive arts therapy: Brain, body, and imagination in the healing process.* Guilford Press.

Malik, F., & Marwaha, R. (2023). *Cognitive development.* StatPearls. https://www.ncbi.nlm.nih.gov/books/NBK537095/

Maynard, B. R., Farina, A., Dell, N. A., & Kelly, M. S. (2019). Effects of trauma-informed approaches in schools: A systematic review. *Campbell Systematic Reviews, 15*(1–2), e1018. https://doi.org/10.1002/cl2.1018

McClymont, J. (2023). *The therapeutic power of collage: A creative path to alleviating anxiety.* National Council of Integrative Psychotherapists. https://reflectonacademy.co.uk/wp-content/uploads/sites/1969/2024/02/The_Therapeutic_Power_of_Collage_-_A_Creative_Path_to_Alleviating_Anxiety_part1.pdf

Morison, L., Simonds, L., & Stewart, S.-J. F. (2022). Effectiveness of creative arts–based interventions for treating children and adolescents exposed to traumatic events: A systematic review of the quantitative evidence and meta-analysis. *Arts & Health, 14*(3), 237–262. https://doi.org/10.1080/17533015.2021.2009529

Owens, E., & Parsons, R. (2025). *Crisis and trauma counseling: Unique forms of helping* (2nd ed.). Cognella.

Pifalo, T. (2007). Jogging the cogs: Trauma-focused art therapy and cognitive behavioral therapy with sexually abused children. *Art Therapy, 24*(4), 170–175. https://doi.org/10.1080/07421656.2007.10129471

Rubin, J. A. (2016). *Approaches to art therapy: Theory and technique* (3rd ed.). Routledge.

Saunders, B. E., & Adams, Z. W. (2014). Epidemiology of traumatic experiences in childhood. *Child and Adolescent Psychiatric Clinics of North America, 23*(2), 167–184.

Singh, C., Sirekha, C., & Jaishree, K. (2023). Efficacy of mandala coloring intervention on executive functioning and emotional & motivational self-regulation among children with symptoms of attention deficit hyperactivity disorder. *Cureus, 15*(10), e46919. https://doi.org/10.7759/cureus.46919

Støre, S. J., & Jakobsson, N. (2022). The effect of mandala coloring on state anxiety: A systematic review and meta-analysis. *Art Therapy, 39*(4), 173–181. https://doi.org/10.1080/07421656.2021.2003144

Substance Abuse and Mental Health Services Administration (SAMHSA; 2023). *Child trauma.* Substance Abuse and Mental Health Services Administration. https://www.samhsa.gov/mental-health/trauma-violence/child-trauma

Van Lith, T., Quintero, A., Pizzutto, E., & Grzywacz, J. G. (2018). "Vamos a la Escuelita Arte Terapia": An art therapy protocol for promoting resilience with Latino farm worker children. *Journal of Infant, Child, and Adolescent Psychotherapy, 17*(3), 213–228. https://doi.org/10.1080/15289168.2018.1490068

Woollett, N., Bandeira, M., & Hatcher, A. (2020). Trauma-informed art and play therapy: Pilot study outcomes for children and mothers in domestic violence shelters in the United States and South Africa. *Child Abuse & Neglect, 107,* 104564. https://doi.org/10.1016/j.chiabu.2020.104564

Zeevi L. S. (2021). Making art therapy virtual: Integrating virtual reality into art therapy with adolescents. *Frontiers in Psychology, 12,* 584943. https://doi.org/10.3389/fpsyg.2021.584943

IMAGE CREDITS

Fig. 6.1: AnonMoos, "Flower of Life," https://commons.wikimedia.org/wiki/File:Flower-of-Life-19circles36arcs-enclosed.png, 2005.

Fig. 6.2: Generated using ChatGPT.

Fig. 6.3: Generated using ChatGPT.

CHAPTER 7

Service Members Experiencing Trauma and PTSD

Whether labeled with the Civil War term *soldier's heart*, World War I's *shell shock*, or World War II's *combat fatigue*, veterans and military personnel have long known and experienced the devastation of post-traumatic stress disorder (PTSD). PTSD affects up to 11.7% of US veterans, a number that is significant given that the rate of PTSD in the civilian population is about 6% (Schein et al., 2021).

While the need for intervention is obvious, mental health providers working with military personnel and veterans have reported a lack of engagement, high dropout rates, and incomplete remission of PTSD when employing the more traditional empirically supported talk therapies (Malhotra et al., 2024). In response, there has been an increasing interest in employing art therapy as a stand-alone approach or, more often, as a supplement to these evidence-based modalities (DeLucia & Kennedy, 2021; Schnitzer et al., 2021).

This chapter reviews the unique needs and challenges presented by military personnel and veterans combating PTSD and the specific models and strategies of art therapy that are effective in treating this population. Upon completion of this chapter, readers will be able to:

1. Describe the unique cultural factors found in the military that can interfere with engagement in therapy for PTSD;
2. Explain the benefits of employing art therapy with service members combating PTSD;
3. Describe the use and benefits of employing mask-making, montage-creating, and containment artwork when working with service members with PTSD.

PTSD in Military Cultural Context

Military personnel and veterans face a higher risk of developing PTSD compared to civilians due to exposure to combat, life-threatening situations, and moral injury (i.e., a profound psychological impact from acting against deeply held moral values or witnessing others do so during combat). Despite advances in understanding PTSD and its treatment, many service members and veterans do not seek care or become early dropouts of the most commonly used PTSD psychotherapies (Amsalem et al., 2021).

It appears that the military culture and values play a critical role in shaping attitudes and behaviors around mental health, often discouraging help-seeking (Meyer et al., 2023).

Military culture is rooted in values such as stoicism and self-sacrifice. These values, while helpful when engaged in conflict, can, for service members struggling with PTSD, interfere with seeking, receiving, and engaging in therapy (Beech et al., 2024). Resistance to engaging with therapy is fueled by the military culture's judgment of a mental disorder as a personal weakness and/or something service members should have control over (Nash et al., 2009).

Military personnel are trained to be mentally and physically fit and resilient in adversity. However, military culture rejects weakness, and seeking psychological treatment is often associated with personal weakness (Denning et al., 2014). Therefore, military personnel concerned that their emotional struggles will be viewed as weaknesses may avoid seeking treatment and conceal their symptoms (Fox et al., 2015).

While cultural understanding and sensitivity is essential for all mental health practitioners regardless of the client population served, it is particularly vital for any mental health provider working with service members. Understanding the nature of the military culture and the unique challenges it presents to the treatment of those with PTSD is a must if one is to have any hope of being effective (Meyer et al., 2016).

Art Therapy: Facilitating Disclosure

As is true for treating civilians with PTSD, the recommended treatment for military personnel and veterans includes prolonged exposure, cognitive behavioral therapy, and cognitive processing therapy (Williamson et al., 2021). While these strategies are effective (Haagen et al., 2015), there is a significant rate of dropout for veterans engaged in trauma-focused PTSD treatment (Imel et al., 2013).

It has been proposed (e.g., Litz et al., 2009) that one factor contributing to the resistance to seek and remain in treatment is that many military personnel and veterans with PTSD often experience moral injury (i.e., reactions to engaging in or witnessing transgressions of deeply held moral beliefs). The guilt and shame associated with moral injury may inhibit an individual's willingness to disclose their experience (Farnsworth et al., 2014). This reluctance to communicate would interfere with the dynamics of typical talking therapies (Schnitzer et al., 2022). Additionally, it is felt that unresolved moral injury may support the continuation of PTSD symptoms despite the use of evidence-based PTSD treatments (Jones et al., 2020).

It has been suggested that art therapy represents a less threatening approach to processing strong feelings, including guilt and shame (Williamson et al., 2021). Art therapy creates a safe space where emotional expression is encouraged (Czamanski-Cohen & Weihs, 2023). Trauma survivors find it less threatening to retell their memories through pictures and visual symbolism than to speak about them (Harris, 2009). During art therapy sessions, clients can safely and nonverbally express what is inside and practice managing overwhelming emotions by directing them to visual creative outputs (Jones et al., 2018).

The creative process allows individuals to access unconscious material, gain insights into their experiences, and reclaim agency over their narratives (Gantt & Vesprini, 2017; Malchiodi, 2020). As such, art therapy or inclusion of art as an intervention may serve as a suitable alternative or supplement to traditional interventions when working with military veterans with PTSD (Walker et al., 2017). In addition to facilitating client awareness and release of painful experiences, the client's artwork provides the therapist and the client with a focal point for therapeutic processing and the development of a new perspective and reconstruction of the client's concept of self, others, and the world (Campbell et al., 2016; Spiegel et al., 2006).

Therapeutic Activities

Art therapy has been utilized as a treatment method for military service members experiencing PTSD as part of a multidisciplinary approach at the National Intrepid Center of Excellence (NICoE) at the Walter Reed National Military Medical Center in Bethesda, Maryland (Jones et al., 2018). The therapists working at NICoE often employ mask-making, montage creations, and containment art as strategies to engage service members in their PTSD therapy (Walker, 2017).

Mask-Making

When working with veterans with PTSD, employment of "trauma masks" has been found to assist the veteran in visualizing and communicating the effects of combat-related trauma and build a sense of self-efficacy and normalization (Sargent et al., 2013). Engaging in mask-making allows service members to focus on their own traumatic experience and externalize it with safety and psychological distance. Walker and colleagues (2017) studied 307 masks created by active-duty service members. They reported that mask-making allowed them to express aspects of identity, using symbols related to moral injuries, grief, loss, and a perceived disconnection with society.

The creation of a personalized "trauma mask" helps service members communicate the effects of their service-related trauma. According to Girija Kaimal (2017): "To see the masks is to 'see' the very real impact of post-traumatic stress disorder (PTSD) and traumatic brain injury (TBI) and understand how it impacts the service members' personal lives, relationships, and perceptions of their role in the world."

There is no right or wrong way to create a mask. Clients can use paint, color markers, fabric, cut-out pictures, or any art supplies to decorate their mask. Mask-making can be used in various ways depending on the nature of the objectives and goals of the intervention.

Open-Ended or Structured

As a therapeutic activity, mask-making can be structured or open-ended. Usually made from papier-mâché, a mask is typically provided in either approach. Providing the "blank" mask can reduce a client's anxiety about creating or crafting a mask from scratch.

When employed in an open-ended, nondirective fashion, clients would be given the blank mask and various art materials. They would be told that there are no themes, content directives, or restrictions and that they can decorate any portion of the mask, inside or outside (Lobban et al., 2018).

In a structured approach, clients would create a mask reflecting a specific theme or area of concern. A therapist might invite a client to create a mask representing the "face" they show the world, versus the face of their private self. Or, the client could develop a mask that reflected their inner conflict with the face of the mask divided in half. Or, as illustrated in Figure 7.1, the mask could reflect a person's transition from pre- to post-trauma (Walker, 2017). In this case, the client was asked to represent how they see themselves now, in contrast to the "them" before deployment.

FIGURE 7.1 Me: Before and After

As noted, making the mask provides a safe way to engage with the traumatic experience. The artwork created can act as powerful starting points for conversations about topics and subject matter that the client had previously been unable to verbalize (Walker, 2017). This was true for the client who created Figure 7.1.

When looking at his creation, the client explained, "If you ask my friends or coworkers, they will describe the old me as Mr. Happy, smiling, light-hearted, and upbeat. Now ... not so much. I try to keep it all in and act like the old me, but truthfully, there are times when I feel dark and evil—ashamed of what I observed in my deployment."

While mask-making can be therapeutic, its real value lies in its impact on the client, which increases recognition and willingness to discuss the trauma. Seeing the masks is to "see" the very real impact of post-traumatic stress disorder (Kaimal, 2017). Processing the meaning reflected in the mask can lead to a client's engagement in therapy and rewriting their narrative.

Montage

A montage is a technique to combine several visual elements, for example, preprinted pictures, photos, film, texts, and more traditional art materials (e.g., paint, markers) into a single composition that conveys a narrative or some specific point of relevance to the client. A montage can be a consolidated yet complex visual reflection of clients' experiences (Berberian et al., 2019).

When used in art therapy, as at NICoE, a montage painting can symbolically represent the client's experience. The materials used can be selected to allow the client to be progressively exposed to and integrate traumatic themes. The artwork produced will facilitate the externalizing and processing of these experiences (Berberian et al., 2019).

By juxtaposing disconnected visual forms and images, a client's montage can help them gain new insights and meanings (Raffaelli & Hartzell, 2016). Additionally, the layering of images on a contained surface is believed to encourage the integration of fragmented traumatic experiences of past, present, and future impact of that experience (Jones et al., 2018). With the help and support of the therapist, the "meaning" of the elements in the montage and the overall theme can be examined and processed as they may reflect a client's current experience, sense of identity, or even desired transition to a future state (Walker, 2017).

The art therapist working with service members at NICoE will introduce the activity as a way to give form to their often nonlinear, layered narrative (Walker, 2017). Service members will be given a canvas, sometimes as large as 8' x 10' (Berberian et al., 2019), and be invited to choose to paint first and then collage to embellish, or collage first and embellish with paint, or even go back and forth adding to the layers. In their instructions, Jones and associates (2018) explain:

> There are two different ways to approach this, you can either have an idea in your mind of exactly what you want it to look like and you can spend the session actualizing that image, or you can have no idea of what you want it to look like, no idea what you want it to be about and spend some time going through magazines, cutting out any words or images that resonate with you for whatever reason. It can be insightful to organize what you've collected onto your canvas. (3)

The themes suggested reflect the specific goal of the intervention and may include a view of self or a representation of the passage of time or the challenges and goals they are experiencing (Walker, 2017). Figure 7.2 is a montage created by a service member treated at NICoE (Jones et al., 2018). The montage is visually divided, reflecting the felt delineation between what is being experienced (i.e., the negatives) and what is desired (i.e., relief). As described by Jones and colleagues (2018), the montage represents a box that has ruptured from the pressure of keeping negative words, feelings, and images inside, as well as the large, winding green arrow, which is the NICoE logo accompanied by words of hope and healing. The details montage created by a client provides a meaningful focal point for the therapist-client to pursue.

FIGURE 7.2 Inside and Out—A Montage

Containment Art—Increasing Psychological Safety

While the goal when treating those with PTSD is to assist them in revisiting, reframing, and reprocessing their experience, it is crucial *not* to overwhelm them or retraumatize them through this process. It has been stressed that therapists create a safe environment (e.g., Avrahami, 2006) and employ strategies that can give clients grounding and a sense of safety if memories and emotions become overwhelming (Mehlomakulu, 2019).

Using the metaphor of a container, clients can be "tasked" with creating an image or artwork that can symbolically hold overwhelming emotions, thoughts, and flashbacks (Drass, 2015). The "container," which can be of any design (e.g., a box, a room, circles), can allow the specific elements of the experience to be brought into therapy while at the same time keeping them detached and the client safe until ready to address them directly (Mehlomakulu, 2019). When used in therapy, the client would identify their metaphor for the containment of the elements of their traumatic experience. During distressing memory or visualization, the client can mentally ground and visualize placing the distress away in the container (Mehlomakulu, 2019).

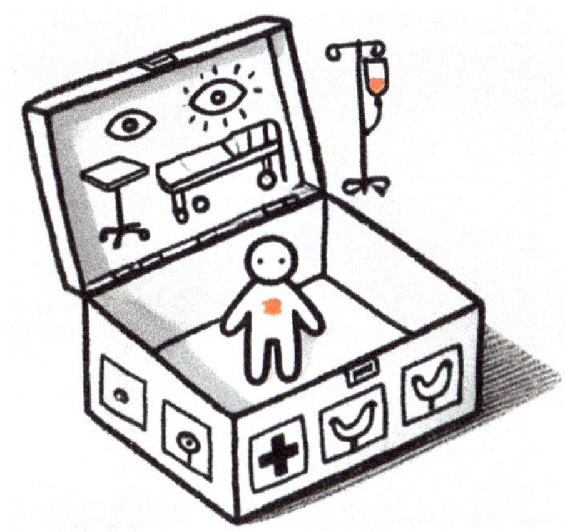

FIGURE 7.3A I Failed

Figure 7.3 represents the creation of one service member's container. The client, a 35-year-old veteran who served as a medical assistant in Afghanistan during Operation Enduring Freedom, was in the operation theatre when her friend was brought in as a result of triggering an improvised explosive device (IED). The container shown in Figure 7.3a houses her memories of the operational theatre, the eyes staring at her, and the blood-stained gown of her friend.

Detaching and symbolically placing her memory of the scene in which her friend died within the container provided some relief when the memory and image were too upsetting to process. The client found additional "escape" from these upsetting and intrusive images and a sense of empowerment by creating a second container with a closed lid and a reminder that she and her friend could "Rest in Peace" (Figure 7.3b).

FIGURE 7.3B Rest in Peace

While the therapeutic goal remained to address this issue, for now, the container provided the client with a sense of control over their traumatic materials, which in future sessions would be revisited and reprocessed.

Effectiveness

Art therapy has been used with various military populations with reported benefits (DeLucia & Kennedy, 2021; Jones et al., 2017; Schnitzer et al., 2021). Most supportive research is of a case study methodology with few randomized control trials (RCTs) being reported.

Campbell et al. (2016) contrasted the impact of cognitive processing therapy (CPT) with CPT in conjunction with art therapy. The researchers employed a randomized controlled study and found a statistically significant greater reduction in PTSD Checklist-Military (PCL-M) scores and the Beck Depression Inventory-II (BDI-II) scores, as well as the increased perceived benefit of treatment, were found in those who received art therapy in addition to CPT. An unexpected finding was that none of the participants in the experimental group dropped out of treatment, whereas 40% of those randomized to CPT alone left treatment prematurely. The dropout rate of the control group is consistent with a recent meta-analysis that showed a dropout rate for PTSD psychotherapies of 36% overall (Goetter et al., 2015).

These results found further support in the work by Decker and colleagues (2018). This research group reported findings of a randomized study of military service members receiving CPT with adjunctive art therapy utilizing a multidirective, visual trauma narrative approach treatment, compared to individuals receiving CPT and supportive psychotherapy. The researchers reported statistically significant improvements in the reduction of PTSD symptoms and depression of those service members receiving CPT plus the adjunctive art therapy. Additionally, the participants experiencing the art therapy rated art therapy as more beneficial than CPT.

Finally, in their review of the literature, Lobban and Murphy (2019) concluded that art therapy has particular value in overcoming PTSD-related avoidance symptoms, increasing self-awareness, and assisting veterans to understand and communicate their inner experiences.

From Knowledge to Application

When used in therapy, creating a mask or montage can provide a therapist and client with valuable insight into the client's experiences and serve as a point of engagement. However, one need not be in therapy to experience the impact of art therapy, specifically the creation of a personal montage.

Creating a montage can facilitate introspection and offer insights into one's view of self and the world and one's emotions and experiences, which may be overlooked or not fully experienced or expressed. You are invited to experience the impact of creating a montage. Exercise 7.1 invites you to explore and reflect on your life journey by visually representing your past, present, and desired future selves.

EXERCISE 7.1 Me: Then—Now—and Someday

Directions:

Step 1: Gather the following materials to create a three-part collage of the you then, the you now, and the hoped-for you of the future.

- Scissors
- Glue sticks
- Colored paper or cardstock (three large sheets)
- Markers, crayons, or colored pencils
- Stickers, embellishments, or other decorative items
- Pictures, words, phrases from magazines, newspapers, or printed images
- (Optional) Personal photos or special mementos

Step 2: Reflect upon the you as a teen, the current you, and the aspired-to-be you. For each of these three phases of life, identify (and list) your strengths, challenges, goals, and views of yourself and the world.

Step 3: Using three sheets of paper or cardstock and the other materials gathered, create a montage reflecting each of these periods of development (your past, present, and future).

Step 4: Process: Place the three sheets of paper in sequence from the past to the future and respond to the following.

- What, if anything, surprised you during this exercise?
- What common themes, strengths, or concerns appear to cross from then to now and into the future?
- How did it feel to explore your past, present, and future selves?
- What insights did you gain about your journey to this point?
- What was your experience (i.e., physical and emotional) while creating your montage?
- What are your thoughts about the use of the exercise with your clients?

The Takeaway

Veterans and military personnel encounter unique challenges when dealing with PTSD. Factors such as combat exposure, life-threatening situations, and moral injury contribute to the elevated rates of incidence as compared to the civilian population. Military culture, which emphasizes resilience and stoicism, often discourages seeking help and can worsen avoidance behaviors. Although traditional trauma-focused psychotherapies are effective for many, they face high dropout rates and limited success in this population, often because veterans struggle to verbalize their experiences and emotions.

Art therapy has emerged as a powerful complementary or alternative approach to address these challenges. Through creative methods such as mask-making, montage creation, and symbolic containment, veterans can express emotions and process traumatic memories in a nonverbal, less-threatening manner. Studies have shown the effectiveness of integrating art therapy with evidence-based modalities like cognitive processing therapy (CPT), leading to reduced PTSD symptoms, lower dropout rates, and improved treatment satisfaction.

Keystones

- PTSD affects up to 11.7% of U.S. veterans, nearly double the rate in civilians.
- Military culture, emphasizing stoicism and resilience, often discourages help-seeking, contributing to high dropout rates and incomplete remission with traditional talk therapies.
- Moral injury—shame or guilt from violating deeply held moral beliefs—further complicates PTSD treatment by inhibiting disclosure.
- Art therapy offers a nonthreatening, creative outlet for expressing emotions and memories, making it particularly effective for veterans resistant to traditional therapies.
- Mask-making allows veterans to externalize trauma, using masks to represent emotions, moral injuries, and personal transformations.
- Montage creation combining images and symbols to explore identity, life transitions, and stressors can help integrate fragmented traumatic experiences and promote conscious reflection with therapeutic guidance.
- Creating symbolic containers to "hold" overwhelming emotions and memories provides a sense of control and psychological safety.
- Art therapy shows promise in reducing PTSD symptoms, increasing self-awareness, and improving engagement with trauma-focused therapies.

ADDITIONAL RESOURCES

Berberian, M., Walker, M. S., & Kaimal, G. (2019). "Master my demons": Art therapy montage paintings by active-duty military service members with traumatic brain injury and post-traumatic stress. *Medical Humanities*, 45(4), 353–360. https://doi.org/10.1136/medhum-2018-011493

Bills, L. (n.d.). *About trauma art narrative therapy*. https://learn.lakesidetraining.org/wp-content/uploads/2024/08/About-Trauma-Art-Narrative-Therapy.pdf

Howie, P. (Ed.). (2017). *Art therapy with military populations: History, innovation, and applications*. Routledge.

National Intrepid Center of Excellence Center. https://health.mil/Military-Health-Topics/Centers-of-Excellence/NICOE

U.S. Department of Veteran Affairs, National Center for PTSD. (n.d.). *Learn about PTSD from veterans who've been there*. About Face. https://www.ptsd.va.gov/apps/aboutface/

REFERENCES

Amsalem, D., Lazarov, A., Markowitz, J. C., Naiman, A., Smith, T. E., Dixon, L. B., & Neria, Y. (2021). Psychiatric symptoms and moral injury among US healthcare workers in the COVID-19 era. *BMC Psychiatry, 21*(1), 546. https://doi.org/10.1186/s12888-021-03565-9

Avrahami, D. (2006). Visual art therapy's unique contribution in the treatment of post-traumatic stress disorders. *Journal of Trauma & Dissociation, 6*(4), 5–38. doi:10.1300/j229v06n04_02

Beech, E.H., Mackey, K.M., Parr, N.J., Baltich, N. B., Young, S., Belsher, B.E. (2024). *Moral Injury and Mental Health Among US Military Service Members and Veterans: A Systematic Review and Evidence Overview.* Washington, DC: Evidence Synthesis Program, Health Systems Research, Office of Research and Development, Department of Veterans Affairs. VA ESP Project #09-199; 2024.

Berberian, M., Walker, M. S., & Kaimal, G. (2019). "Master My Demons": Art therapy montage paintings by active-duty military service members with traumatic brain injury and post-traumatic stress. *Medical humanities, 45*(4), 353–360.

Campbell, M., Decker, K. P., Kruk, K., & Deaver, S. P. (2016). Art therapy and cognitive processing therapy for combat-related PTSD: A randomized controlled trial. *Art Therapy: Journal of the American Art Therapy Association, 33*(4), 169–177. https://doi.org/10.1080/07421656.2016.1226643

Czamanski-Cohen, J., & Weihs, K. L. (2023). The role of emotion processing in art therapy (REPAT) intervention protocol. *Frontiers in Psychology, 14*, 1208901. https://doi.org/10.3389/fpsyg.2023.1208901

Decker, K. P., Deaver, S. P., Abbey, V., Campbell, M., & Turpin, C. (2018). Quantitatively improved treatment outcomes for combat-associated PTSD with adjunctive art therapy: Randomized controlled trial. *Art Therapy, 35*(4), 184–194.

DeLucia, J., & Kennedy, B. (2021). A veteran-focused art therapy program: Co-research to strengthen art therapy effectiveness. *International Journal of Art Therapy 26*, 8–16. doi: 10.1080/17454832.2021.1889007

Denning, L. A., Meisnere, M., & Warner, K. E. (Eds.). (2014). *Preventing psychological disorders in service members and their families: An assessment of programs.* National Academies Press.

Drass, J. M. (2015). Art therapy for individuals with borderline personality: Using a dialectical behavior therapy framework. *Art Therapy, 32*(4), 168–176.

Farnsworth, J. K., Drescher, K. D., Nieuwsma, J. A., Walser, R. B., & Currier, J. M. (2014). The role of moral emotions in military trauma: Implications for the study and treatment of moral injury. *Review of General Psychology, 18*(4), 249–262, https://doi.org/10.1037/gpr0000018

Fox, A. B., Meyer, E. C., & Vogt, D. (2015). Attitudes about the VA health-care setting, mental illness, and mental health treatment and their relationship with VA mental health service use among female and male OEF/OIF veterans. *Psychological Services, 12*(1), 49–58. https://doi.org/10.1037/a0038269

Gantt, L., & Vesprini, M. E. (2017). Using the instinctual trauma response model in a military setting. In P. Howie (Ed.), *Art therapy with military populations: History, innovation, and applications* (pp. 147–156). Routledge.

Goetter, E. M., Bui, E., Ojserkis, R. A., Zakarian, R. J., Brendel, R. W., & Simon, N. M. (2015). A systematic review of dropout from psychotherapy for posttraumatic stress disorder among Iraq and Afghanistan combat veterans. *Journal of Traumatic Stress, 28*(5), 401–409.

Haagen, J. F. G., Smid, G. E., Knipscheer, J. W., & Kleber, R. J. (2015). The efficacy of recommended treatments for veterans with PTSD: A meta-regression analysis. *Clinical Psychology Review, 40*, 184–194. https://doi.org/10.1016/j.cpr.2015.06.008

Harris, D. A. (2009). The paradox of expressing speechless terror: Ritual liminality in the creative arts therapies' treatment of posttraumatic distress. *The Arts in Psychotherapy, 36*(2), 94–104.

Imel, Z. E., Laska, K., Jakupcak, M., and Simpson, T. L. (2013). Meta-analysis of dropout in treatments for posttraumatic stress disorder. *Journal of Consulting and Clinical Psychology 81*, 394–404. doi: 10.1037/a0031474

Jones, C., Smith-Macdonald, L., Miguel-Cruz, A., Lentz, L., Pike, A., & Brémault-Phillips, S. (2020). Tackling trauma with technology: Treating chronic combat-related PTSD in Canadian Armed Forces personnel and Veterans with 3MDR. *Annual Review of CyberTherapy and Telemedicine, 18*, 235–239.

Jones, J. P., Walker, M. S., Drass, J. M., & Kaimal, G. (2018). Art therapy interventions for active duty military service members with post-traumatic stress disorder and traumatic brain injury. *International Journal of Art Therapy, 23*(2), 70–85. https://doi.org/10.1080/17454832.2017.1388263

Kaimal, G. (2017). *Unmasking the trauma: A look at research on mask making as a creative arts therapy.* National Endowment for the Arts. https://www.arts.gov/stories/blog/2017/unmasking-trauma-look-research-mask-making-creative-arts-therapy

Litz, B. T., Stein, N., Delaney, E., Lebowitz, L., Nash, W. P., Silva, C., & Maguen, S. (2009). Moral injury and moral repair in war veterans: A preliminary model and intervention strategy. *Clinical Psychology Review, 29*(8), 695–706.

Lobban, J., Mackay, K., Redgrave, M., & Rajagopal, S. (2018). An adaptive art therapy model for working with traumatized veterans. In J. Lobban (Ed.), *Art therapy with military veterans: Trauma and the image* (pp. 103–125). Routledge. https://doi.org/10.4324/9781315564197-7

Lobban, J., & Murphy, D. (2019). Understanding the role art therapy can take in treating veterans with chronic post-traumatic stress disorder. *The Arts in Psychotherapy, 62*, 37–44.

Malchiodi, C. A. (2020). *Trauma and expressive arts therapy: Brain, body, and imagination in the healing process.* Guilford Press.

Malhotra, B., Jones, L. C., Spooner, H., Levy, C., Kaimal, G., & Williamson, J. B. (2024). A conceptual framework for a neurophysiological basis of art therapy for PTSD. *Frontiers in Human Neuroscience, 18*, 1351757. https://doi.org/10.3389/fnhum.2024.1351757

Mehlomakulu, C. (2019). *Protective containers—Using art to strengthen the metaphor.* Creativity in therapy. https://creativityintherapy.com/2019/02/protective-containers-using-art-strengthen-metaphor/

Meyer, J. F., Wattenberg, M. S., Kosman, K. A., Budd, M. A., Duffy, M. J., Agrawal, A., Richmond, J. S., Hough, S., Meltzer, B., Schein, A. Z., Poster, M. F., & Bradley, J. C. (2023). Stigma and barriers to care for mental health treatment for military and veteran populations. In C. H. Warner & C. A. Castro (Eds.), *Veteran and military mental health: A clinical manual* (pp. 45–85). Springer. https://doi.org/10.1007/978-3-031-18009-5_4

Meyer, E. G., Writer, B. W., & Brim, W. (2016). The Importance of Military Cultural Competence. *Current Psychiatry Reports, 18*(3), 26. https://doi.org/10.1007/s11920-016-0662-9

Nash, W. P., Silva, C., & Litz, B. (2009). The historic origins of military and veteran mental health stigma and the stress injury model as a means to reduce it. *Psychiatric Annals, 39*(8), 789–794.

Raffaelli, T., & Hartzell, E. (2016). A comparison of adults' responses to collage versus drawing in an initial art-making session. *Art Therapy, 33*(1), 21–26.

Sargent, P. D., Campbell, J. S., Richter, K. E., McLay, R. N., & Koffman, R. L. (2013). Integrative medical practices for combat-related posttraumatic stress disorder. *Psychiatric Annals, 43*(4), 181–187. https://doi.org/10.3928/00485713-20130403-10

Schein, J., Houle, C., Urganus, A., Cloutier, M., Patterson-Lomba, O., Wang, Y., King, S., Levinson, W., Guérin, A. Lefebvre, P, & Davis, L. L. (2021). Prevalence of post-traumatic stress disorder in the United States: A systematic literature review. *Current Medical Research & Opinion, 37*(12), 2151–2161. doi: 10.1080/03007995.2021.1978417

Schnitzer, G., Holttum, S., and Huet, V. (2021). A systematic literature review of the impact of art therapy upon post-traumatic stress disorder. *International Journal of Art Therapy, 26*(4), 147–160. doi:10.1080/17454832.2021.1910719

Schnitzer, G., Holttum, S., & Huet, V. (2022). "My heart on this bit of paper": A grounded theory of the mechanisms of change in art therapy for military veterans. *Journal of Affective Disorders, 297*, 327–337. https://doi.org/10.1016/j.jad.2021.10.049

Spiegel, D., Malchiodi, C., Backos, A., & Collie, K. (2006). Art therapy for combat-related PTSD: Recommendations for research and practice. *Art Therapy, 23*(4), 157–164.

Walker, M. (2017). Art therapy approaches within the National Intrepid Center of Excellence at Walter Reed National Military Medical Center. In P. Howie (Ed.), *Art therapy with military populations: History, innovation, and applications* (pp. 111–123). Routledge.

Walker, M. S., Kaimal, G., Gonzaga, A. M. L., Myers-Coffman, K. A., & DeGraba, T. J. (2017). Active-duty military service members' visual representations of PTSD and TBI in masks. *International Journal of Qualitative Studies on Health and Well-Being, 12*(1), 1267317. https://doi.org/10.1080/17482631.2016.1267317

Williamson, J. B., Jaffee, M. S., & Jorge, R. E. (2021). Posttraumatic stress disorder and anxiety-related conditions. *Continuum, 27*(6), 1738–1763. doi: 10.1212/con. 0000000000001054

IMAGE CREDITS

Fig. 7.1: Generated using ChatGPT.

Fig. 7.2: Jacqueline P. Jones et al., "Art Therapy Interventions for Active Duty Military Service Members with Post-Traumatic Stress Disorder and Traumatic Brain Injury," *International Journal of Art Therapy*, vol. 23, no. 2, https://doi.org/10.1080/17454832.2017.1388263. Copyright © 2018 by Taylor & Francis Group.

Fig. 7.3a: Generated using ChatGPT.

Fig. 7.3b: Generated using ChatGPT.

CHAPTER 8

Victims of Intimate Partner Violence (IPV)

Intimate partner violence (IPV), a subset of domestic abuse, refers to behavior, including acts of physical aggression, sexual coercion, psychological abuse, and controlling behaviors, within an intimate relationship that causes physical, sexual, or psychological harm (World Health Organization, n.d.). IPV need not be restricted to domestic settings and can occur outside of traditional domestic contexts, such as between dating partners who do not cohabitate. Victims of intimate partner violence often experience post-traumatic stress disorder (PTSD) with intrusive memories, emotional dysregulation, hyperarousal, and a profound sense of helplessness.

Art therapy, with its nonverbal and creative approaches, offers victims a unique way to express and process trauma, enabling them to reconnect with their emotions and reclaim their identities. The current chapter discusses the impact of IPV and techniques that make art therapy an effective approach for treating victims of intimate partner violence and domestic abuse. Upon completion of the chapter, readers will be able to:

1. Describe the nature and impact of intimate partner violence;
2. Explain the unique value of art therapy in the treatment of victims of intimate partner violence, and;
3. Describe three strategies often employed in art therapy when working with victims of intimate partner violence.

Intimate Partner Violence (IPV)

According to the National Center for Injury Prevention and Control (Leemis, 2022), over 61 million women and 53 million men have experienced psychological aggression by an intimate partner in their lifetime. IPV disproportionately affects women, with global estimates suggesting that nearly one in three women experience IPV during their lifetime (WHO, 2021). Men, while also victims, are less likely to report abuse due to social stigmas; as a result, such statistics reflecting incidence of male victims may be underestimates (Hines & Douglas, 2010).

The CDC (2024) identified four types of IPV:

- *Physical violence*—Hurting or trying to hurt a partner with physical force, such as hitting, punching, beating, choking, hitting, kicking, burning, grabbing, pinching, shoving, slapping, hair-pulling, biting, denying medical care, forcing alcohol and/or drug use, or using other physical force.

- *Sexual violence*—Forcing a partner or attempting to force a partner to participate in any sexual act, including nonphysical acts such as sexting, without consent.
- *Stalking*—Repeated, unwanted attention and/or contact by a partner that causes concern for one's safety. This may be via phone, text, mail, or in person. Typical stalking activities include repeated telephone calls, unwelcome letters or gifts by mail, and surveillance at work, home, and other places that the victim is known to frequent.
- *Psychological (mental/emotional) violence*—Verbal or nonverbal communication with the intent to harm another mentally or emotionally to exert control over the other person. The actions can include threatening physical harm to self, partner, or children; destruction of pets and property; "mind games"; or forcing isolation from friends, family, school, and/or work. The abuser undermines the victim's sense of self-worth through constant criticism, name-calling, or other verbal abuse.

When the violence is ongoing, it can induce feelings of shock, disbelief, confusion, terror, isolation, and despair and can undermine a person's sense of self (Owens & Parsons, 2025). Survivors of IPV often experience PTSD, which manifests as intrusive thoughts, nightmares, flashbacks, emotional numbness, and difficulty regulating emotions (Wessells & Kostelny, 2022).

Studies show that nearly 64% of women who experience IPV develop PTSD symptoms, and many continue to struggle with feelings of helplessness, fear, and shame (Dutton et al., 2006). Survivors may become hypervigilant, avoiding situations or people that remind them of their abuser, while others may experience dissociation, struggling to remain present or connected with their surroundings. For these individuals, the abuse disrupts their sense of safety, trust, and identity, creating lasting psychological scars that affect their ability to form healthy relationships or engage in daily activities (see Case Illustration 8.1).

CASE ILLUSTRATION 8.1 Zoe

Zoe, a 29-year-old survivor of IPV, was diagnosed with PTSD after enduring years of emotional and physical abuse. Zoe was married at the age of 17. At the time, she was pregnant and lost the baby as a result of a beating by her boyfriend, the father of the child and eventually her husband. The relationship was one marked by physical and psychological abuse.

Zoe's husband was an alcoholic who would rage when he was intoxicated. During these times, he became verbally abusive, often sexually abusive (i.e., demanding sexual acts that Zoe did not want), and when rebuffed, would punch and kick Zoe. The last incident of physical abuse resulted in Zoe being hospitalized with multiple cuts, bruises, and a concussion. While she refused to press charges, she was able, with the support of the hospital social worker, to leave her husband and file for divorce.

While the divorce, which was finalized two years prior to her current engagement in therapy, ended the actual abuse and violence, it did not end her pain and suffering. Zoe entered therapy as a result of experiencing debilitating flashbacks of her partner's violence. She has withdrawn from many social contacts and situations in fear of encountering him, and when out in public, she has become hypervigilant and often experiences extreme anxiety. Her fears and avoidant behaviors have grown to the point where she is losing friendships and is in danger of being let go from her work.

A Creative Approach to Healing PTSD Resulting from IPV

Art therapy, with its creative and expressive nature, has emerged as a powerful tool in the healing process for those with PTSD as a result of IPV. Art therapy offers survivors an opportunity and means to express and process their trauma in a nonverbal, safe, and supportive space (Binkley, 2013). Art-making allows individuals to externalize emotions that may be too overwhelming or difficult to articulate with words, regulate emotions and behaviors, enhance self-esteem, reduce anxiety, and gain awareness of other healthy self-aspects beyond their survivor self-aspects (Ikonomopoulos et al., 2017).

Techniques such as mandala drawing/coloring, collage-making, and clay work empower IPV survivors to take control of their narrative, reclaim identity and agency, and transform their experiences from sources of shame or fear into symbols of strength and growth.

Mandala Drawing and Coloring: Finding Center Amid Chaos

The creation or coloring of mandalas is commonly used in art therapy (Stinley et al., 2015). Mandala patterns are typically circular and symmetrical in design. The drawing or coloring of the mandala is a task suited to individuals with a trauma history.

The repetitive and rhythmic movement of a pencil or crayon through the design helps the client focus on the now, often providing them with a sense of calm and experience of self-soothing. The use of mandalas with victims of intimate partner violence can help them gradually regain a sense of control and order and reduce PTSD symptoms (Nasiri et al., 2024). The technique is found to evoke a sense of balance, and harmony, and this is helpful for trauma survivors who struggle with emotional dysregulation (Duong et al., 2018).

It is felt that focusing on intricate designs and patterns helps ground a client in the moment (Hosseini & Borzabadi Farahani, 2022). This can prove helpful in moments of overwhelming anxiety or intrusive thoughts (Babouchkina & Robbins, 2015; Lee, 2018). Further, drawing and coloring mandalas help clients become aware of their thoughts and feelings, increasing their mindfulness and emotional self-regulation (Duong et al., 2018).

The Process

The use of mandala drawing or coloring as an intervention is not manualized or standardized in some step-by-step procedure. But as is true for any intervention employed in therapy, the first step would be to provide the client with an overview of the mandala's purpose and the specific value of its employment within their therapy. Assuming client consent, the therapist could then proceed to the client with a predesigned mandala (e.g., https://mondaymandala.com/m/) or materials, including precut circles upon which they would create their design. Clients would then be provided access to art supplies such as magazines, markers, pencils, crayons, stencils, staples, tape, glue, fabric, and scissors and invited to personalize their mandalas.

If the intervention is unstructured, the client would be encouraged to work with their mandala however they may choose. The intervention can be more directed and structured in order to address a specific issue or theme. In this case, the therapist would provide guidance regarding the creation of a mandala. Clients may be asked to create a mandala that reflects their current emotions, level of felt safety or empowerment, or some other theme or session focus.

The process of creating or coloring a mandala has therapeutic value in that creating or coloring a mandala is not only a grounding activity but it can also facilitate disclosure of difficult emotions and provide a focal point for client-therapist discussion (Henderson et al., 2007). When the process is repeated across session, changes in the artwork can also serve as an indication of the progress and transformation being experienced.

Case Illustration 8.2 highlights mandala coloring as an outlet for emotions and contributes to the client's sense of agency and control. The mandala she created at the end of her therapy (see Figure 8.2) starkly contrasted with her minimalist presentation created during her initial session (see Figure 8.1). In describing her final creation, Portia noted that the mandala had a golden core, reflecting her inner strength and growing belief in her worth and value.

CASE ILLUSTRATION 8.2 Portia

Portia, a 42-year-old mother and homemaker, recently separated from her husband of 21 years. As she noted at the time of her first therapy session, she has been a victim of verbal and sexual humiliation by her husband since they got married. She endured this abuse for the sake of her son, who now is grown and has left the home. His independence provided her the freedom to do the same, but she recognizes how much she has bought into her husband's abusive messages, and she doubts her worth and ability to make it on her own.

During her first session, she explained how anxious she was and how concerned she was about "messing up and making a mistake." In response to her disclosure, the therapist suggested that she engage in activity that many have reported to be calming. The therapist explained the nature of the mandala activity and provided Portia with a predesigned mandala and invited her to color it to reflect how she felt at the moment. Portia took the preprinted mandala and colored it with a subdued color palette (see Figure 8.1). When asked about her mandala, she noted that she was feeling anxious and concerned about doing something wrong so she chose what she felt was a safe, minimalistic, yet expressive pattern with a subdued color palette that would be nonoffensive.

Through therapy, her initial feelings of anxiety, self-depreciation, and impotence gave way to a realistic self-evaluation and belief in her resiliency and value as a person. This transformation was evident in the mandala she colored at her next-to-last therapy session (see Figure 8.2).

FIGURE 8.1 Cautious

FIGURE 8.2 Bright and Beautiful

Collage-Making: Reconstructing One's Self

Collage-making involves combining images, textures, and words from magazines, photographs, or other materials to create a visual narrative. The process focuses on selecting materials and cutting them into the desired shape before arranging them and pasting them onto the chosen surface (Rise Art, n.d.).

This technique helps clients to integrate painful experiences without overwhelming themselves. The materials employed can trigger emotions and enable the client to access their traumatic memories (Spiegel et al., 2006). The selection and arrangement of images allow for the externalization of internal states, aiding in processing traumatic experiences (Schouten et al., 2015).

When creating a collage, it is vital to provide the client with the freedom to choose themes and materials in service of their developing their sense of agency. Such freedom of choice can be empowering and can help to counteract feelings of helplessness that often accompany PTSD (Heijman et al., 2024).

The process arranging and rearranging of the pieces can serve as a symbolic reconstruction of self, helping the client make sense of their experience, reduce the intrusive re-experiencing of the traumatic events, and establishing a sense of self and their world as desired (Babla, 2020). Creating a collage can mirror the client's efforts to piece together fragmented and disjointed memories and in the process reconstruct their experiences into a more cohesive, empowering story (Steele & Malchiodi, 2012). Collage-making can help individuals reclaim their voices, validate their emotions, and visualize their path to recovery (see Case Illustration 8.3).

CASE ILLUSTRATION 8.3 From Fractured Self to Wholeness

Rosalie, a 38-year-old survivor of intimate partner violence, used collage-making to express the fractured sense of self she had developed over years of emotional and physical abuse. In her first collage, Rosalie incorporated torn photographs of herself at different ages, some intact and others shredded or partially obscured. The collage symbolizes her loss of identity during the abusive relationship. She used black-and-white images to represent her emotional numbness and added bright red cutouts to symbolize the intensity of her emotions.

Throughout her therapy, Rosalie began incorporating more vibrant colors to represent moments of self-discovery and strength. Her final collage, "Me as Strong and Beautiful," depicted a series of torn photographs, mostly from fashion magazines, arranged to form a new, unified image of herself, symbolizing her journey from fragmentation to wholeness (see Figure 8.3).

Rosalie knew her journey would continue, but she now believed in herself, her strength, and her resilience. "I'm taking the pieces of myself that felt broken and making something new, beautiful, and strong. I know I have more to do, but I know I can do it."

FIGURE 8.3 Me as Strong and Beautiful

The Process

Babla (2020) suggested a four-step approach to employing collage-making in a therapy session. In preparation, the therapist would need to gather materials for the activity. It is important for the therapist to pay attention to the items selected and provided so that the materials and themes do not overwhelm or retraumatize the client. With materials gathered, the client is invited to review and select things that grabbed their attention. Babla (2020) suggested this *browsing stage* would be followed by the *cutting stage*, during which clients cut or tear specific items and images they intended to use.

Once the materials have been selected, the client would start the *arranging and sticking* stage in a preliminary staging and creation of the collage. During this stage, clients are encouraged to move, adjust, and relocate the items or add and delete certain pieces as they felt. With the pieces moved, placed, and now fixed to a base, the client and therapist enter the *narration phase*. It is at this phase, with focus on the overall impression and the details of the collage, that the therapist helps the client process their experience and identify the meaning of their creation.

Clay Work: Grounding and Connecting

PTSD often results in dissociation or numbing, where survivors feel disconnected from their emotions or their physical selves. Clay is an action-oriented, kinesthetic, and embodied experience, which differs from the processing of emotions in talk-based therapy (Skop et al., 2022).

Touching clay establishes a sensory and emotional connection, aiding in exploring and processing feelings (Elbrecht & Antcliff, 2014). The engagement with the clay invites a range of responses and embodiment of emotions, from gentle touch and soothing to the intense input of physical energy by way of pounding, poking, tossing, rolling, and the like (Nan & Ho, 2017). Nan et al. (2021) considered an interaction with clay a bodily based affective experience that heightens our physical and emotional awareness.

The Process

Once provided with the materials needed (e.g., clay, water, paper towels, a box or plate to place the clay on, etc.), the client may be directed to explore the texture and malleability of the clay without concern for creating a specific form. The employment of clay in therapy can be unstructured—free form—with clients given free rein to sculpt and shape the clay in any way they desire. This allows for uninhibited creative expression. There are no rules or guidelines. The therapist invites the client to explore what the clay feels like and do whatever they desire with it. The physical act of kneading, pounding, or shaping the clay can be cathartic, allowing for the channeling of pent-up emotion. By shaping and molding clay, clients can literally knead out their tensions and reshape the clay to reflect their inner state. The engagement with the clay invites a focused concentration and a quiet mind, which can facilitate the reduction of stress (Kimport & Robbins, 2012).

Clay work can also be structured. For example, clients could be encouraged to create sculptures that symbolically represent their experiences or be invited to create scenes or a narrative that reflect personal stories, memories, or aspirations. A focused task with clay allows a client to externalize abstract concepts or emotions in tangible forms. With the therapist's support, clients can use clay to symbolically work through their experiences by shaping and reshaping them into forms that reflect their inner state or that which they desire.

Using clay when treating those experiencing PTSD has been found to (1) reduce stress and anxiety (Zhang et al., 2024), (2) facilitate the expression of difficult emotions (Sholt & Gavron, 2006), and (3) contribute to the client's reconstruction and self-repair of their identity (Elbrecht, 2021). Case Illustration 8.4 demonstrates the value of clay work in assisting a client to share difficult emotions and establish a desired vision.

CASE ILLUSTRATION 8.4 Raul: Standing Tall

Raul, a 32-year-old accountant, was self-referred to therapy because of his "intense fear of losing control and hurting someone." During the intake session, he disclosed that he is the victim of vicious verbal and, on occasion, physical attacks from his wife of eight years. Raul shared that his wife constantly belittles him, criticizing everything from his appearance to his "failure as a provider" and his "inadequacy" in the bedroom.

This type of verbal abuse is not new to Raul. As a child, he grew up in a household where his mother was also verbally abusive. He shared that he has survived the marriage by "going numb, becoming emotionally invisible," but that lately, he is having difficulty going numb and has had thoughts of hurting his wife.

During the second session, Raul was introduced to clay work and asked to create something representing his feelings about himself. He created a person lying on their side in the fetal position. Discussing his creation, he shared that he saw himself as "a child, one who could not stand up for himself. I cower like a frightened child."

The use of clay work in each session served as a grounding technique, enabling Raul to stay present during emotionally challenging moments in therapy. Over the course of his therapy, Raul began to reframe his self-denigrating thoughts, remove his shame about being a coward, and dismiss his thoughts about being unable to control his emotions, particularly his anger. The transformation of Raul's self-view is evident in his clay work, which he produced at his last therapy session and entitled "Standing Strong and Tall" (Figure 8.4).

FIGURE 8.4 Standing Strong and Tall

Unlike the person escaping to the fetal position, Raul saw himself as competent and assertive even when uncomfortable in a relationship. He realized he could express his feelings and concerns without acting out. His ability to stand tall and discuss his feelings with his wife not only helped her recognize what she was doing but also helped the couple see the need and value of counseling together, a decision they embraced.

From Knowledge to Application

Creative activities like mandala coloring, collage-making, and clay work provide valuable opportunities for self-discovery, emotional release, and insight. As discussed in this chapter, mandala drawing/coloring promotes calm, balance, and grounding. It helps IPV survivors regain a sense of control and reduce PTSD symptoms. Exercise 8.1 invites you to experience the grounding and calming effect of mandala coloring.

EXERCISE 8.1 Mandala Coloring

Mandala coloring is a simple yet powerful tool for fostering relaxation and mindfulness. It helps start a session when working with IPV victims, and experiencing its effects firsthand will help you understand the value of this technique.

Step 1: Preparation

You will need a quiet place to color, a mandala, and some colored crayons, pencils, or markers. You can find over 200 free mandalas that you can download and print at https://mondaymandala.com/m/.

Step 2: Mandala Coloring

As you look through the free mandalas, select one that resonates with you today. Choose colors that reflect your mood or what you feel drawn to. As you color, focus on the mandala, the colors being applied, and your hand motion.

Step 3: Reflection

- How did coloring the mandala make you feel?
- Did focusing on the mandala impact your sense of calm and grounding?
- Did you notice any changes in your breathing, body tension, or thoughts?
- What challenges did you experience in staying present and focused during the activity?
- How might this activity be beneficial for clients in a therapeutic setting?
- How might you adjust this activity to increase its therapeutic value?

Step 4: Next time

The next time you feel somewhat stressed or anxious and have the opportunity to color a mandala, start by creating a subjective unit of discomfort scale (SUDS) where 10 reflects maximum stress and discomfort and 1 represents no noticeable stress or discomfort. Evaluate your level of stress before and following the mandala coloring.

The Takeaway

Art therapy not only helps IPV survivors process trauma and reduce PTSD symptoms but also empowers them to reclaim their narratives and rebuild their identities. Art therapy offers IPV survivors a safe and creative outlet to express their trauma, regulate emotions, and regain a sense of control over their healing process. Through techniques like mandala drawing/coloring, collage making, and clay work, survivors can externalize difficult emotions, reframe their traumatic experiences, and visualize their healing. By engaging in the therapeutic process, victims of intimate partner violence can reconstruct their narratives and, in so doing, rebuild their identities, regaining their sense of autonomy.

Keystones

- *Intimate partner violence (IPV)* includes physical, sexual, and psychological violence and stalking by a current or former partner.
- IPV often results in PTSD symptoms, including intrusive thoughts, hyperarousal, emotional dysregulation, and feelings of helplessness.
- Art therapy provides a nonverbal, creative outlet for expressing trauma. It fosters emotional regulation, self-expression, and the reconstruction of identity.
- Mandala drawing/coloring promotes calm, balance, and grounding and helps survivors regain a sense of control and reduce PTSD symptoms.
- Collage-making facilitates the symbolic reconstruction of fragmented memories into cohesive narratives.
- Clay work provides a tactile, embodied experience that explores emotions, reduces dissociation, and assists clients in reconnecting with their physical and emotional selves.
- The use of art therapy in the IPV context can help clients with emotional healing, empowerment, and identity reconstruction.

ADDITIONAL RESOURCES

Adapted, S. (2024). *Color Your Soul Whole: Overcoming Domestic Violence* (4 books). Author.

Buchalter, S. I. (2009). *Art therapy techniques and applications.* Jessica Kingsley Publishers.

Crocker, T., & Carr, S. M. D. (2021). *Clay work and body image in art therapy: Using metaphor and symbolism to heal.* Routledge.

Elbrecht, C. (2020). Trauma healing at the clay field: A conversation with Cornelia Elbrecht. Institute for Sensorimotor Art Therapy. https://www.sensorimotorarttherapy.com/blog/trauma-healing-at-the-clay-field-a-conversation-with-cornelia-elbrecht?gad_source=1&gad_campaignid=21285928557&gbraid=0AAAABmawI1T9Nfs8pC_TlAvGLDModSwf&gclid=Cj0KCQjw3OjGBhDYARIsADd-uX5p9pWbYMt2BFqkqmGKjM4Eq3PuhIOKO-yxSS3DIr54xJzJsBwmRh4aArZsEALw_wcB

Seager, S. (2023). *Relaxation adult coloring book: Flower mandala style!* Author.

REFERENCES

Babla, A. (2020). *Putting the pieces together: Collage as a mode in treating trauma.* Collage Research Network. https://collageresearchnetwork.wordpress.com/2020/05/29/putting-the-pieces-together-collage-as-a-mode-in-the-treatment-of-trauma/?utm_source=chatgpt.com

Babouchkina, A., & Robbins, S. J. (2015). Reducing negative mood through mandala creation: A randomized controlled trial. *Art Therapy, 32*(1), 34–39. doi: http://dx.doi.org/10.1080/07421656.2015.994428

Binkley, E. (2013). Creative strategies for treating victims of domestic violence. *Journal of Creativity in Mental Health, 8*(3), 305–313.

Centers for Disease Control and Prevention. (2024). *About intimate partner violence.* Centers for Disease Control and Prevention. Retrieved https://www.cdc.gov/intimate-partner-violence/about/?CDC_AAref_Val=https://www.cdc.gov/violenceprevention/intimatepartnerviolence/fastfact.html

Duong, K., Stargell, N. A., & Mauk, G. W. (2018). Effectiveness of coloring mandala designs to reduce anxiety in graduate counseling students. *Journal of Creativity in Mental Health, 13*(3), 318–330.

Dutton, M. A., Green, B. L., Kaltman, S. I., Roesch, D. M., Zeffiro, T. A., & Krause, E. D. (2006). Intimate partner violence, PTSD, and adverse health outcomes. *Journal of Interpersonal Violence, 21*(7), 955–968. https://doi.org/10.1177/0886260506289178

Elbrecht, C. (2021). *Healing trauma in children with Clay Field therapy: How sensorimotor art therapy supports the embodiment of developmental milestones.* North Atlantic Books.

Elbrecht, C., & Antcliff, L. R. (2014). Being touched through touch. Trauma treatment through haptic perception at the Clay Field: A sensorimotor art therapy. *International Journal of Art Therapy, 19*(1), 19–30. https://doi.org/10.1080/17454832.2014.880932

Heijman, J., Wouters, H., Schouten, K. A., & Haeyen, S. (2024). Effectiveness of trauma-focused art therapy (TFAT) for psychological trauma: Study protocol of a multiple-baseline single-case experimental design. *BMJ Open, 14*(1), e081917. https://doi.org/10.1136/bmjopen-2023-081917

Henderson, P., Rosen, D., & Mascaro, N. (2007). Empirical study on the healing nature of mandalas. *Psychology of Aesthetics, Creativity, and the Arts, 1*(3), 148–154. https://doi.org/10.1037/1931-3896.1.3.148

Hines, D. A., & Douglas, E. M. (2010). Intimate terrorism by women towards men: Does it exist? *Journal of Aggression, Conflict and Peace Research, 2*(3), 36–56. https://doi.org/10.5042/jacpr.2010.0335

Hosseini, M., & Borzabadi Farahani, Z. (2022). Evaluating the effectiveness of mandala coloring on mental health in Iran: A systematic review. *Journal of Health Sciences & Surveillance System, 10*(2), 144–149.

Ikonomopoulos, J., Cavazos-Vela, J., Vela, P., Sanchez, M., Schmidt, C., & Catchings, C. V. (2017). Evaluating the effects of creative journal arts therapy for survivors of domestic violence. *Journal of Creativity in Mental Health, 12*(4), 496–512.

Kimport, E. R., & Robbins, S. J. (2012). Efficacy of creative clay work for reducing negative mood: A randomized controlled trial. *Art Therapy, 29*(2), 74–79. https://doi.org/10.1080/07421656.2012.680048

Lee, S.-L. (2018). Why color mandalas? A study of anxiety-reducing mechanisms. *Art Therapy, 35*(1), 35–41. https://doi.org/10.1080/07421656.2018.1459105

Leemis, R. W., Friar, N., Khatiwada, S., Chen, M. S., Kresnow, M., Smith, S. G., Caslin, S., & Basile, K. C. (2022). *The National Intimate Partner and Sexual Violence Survey: 2016/2017 report on intimate partner violence.* National Center for Injury Prevention and Control, Centers for Disease Control and Prevention.

Nan, J. K. M., Hinz, L. D., & Lusebrink, V. B. (2021). Clay art therapy on emotion regulation: Research, theoretical underpinnings, and treatment mechanisms. In C. Martin, L.-A. Hunter, V. B. Patel, V. R. Preedy, & R. Rajendram (Eds.), *Neuroscience of Depression* (pp. 431–443). Elsevier Academic Press.

Nan, J. K. M., & Ho, R. T. H. (2017). Effects of clay art therapy on adult outpatients with major depressive disorder: A randomized controlled trial. *Journal of Affective Disorders, 217,* 237–245. https://doi.org/10.1016/j.jad.2017.04.013

Nasiri, M.-A., Sajadi, S. A., Farsi, Z., & Heidarieh, M. (2024). The effect of mandala coloring and free coloring on the happiness in veterans with post-traumatic stress disorder in the Covid-19 pandemic: A randomized clinical trial. *BMC Psychiatry, 24*(1), 467. https://doi.org/10.1186/s12888-024-05886-x

Owens, E., & Parsons, R. (2025). *Crisis and Trauma Counseling: Unique Forms of Helping* (2nd ed.). Cognella.

Rise Art (n.d.). *A Guide to Collage.* Rise Art. https://www.riseart.com/guide/2371/a-guide-to-collage?srsltid=AfmBOorcuFoKiIhKFdL_NE3gd8-u0odd3gQICCGxXKSjlYH8Q1C10hqx

Schouten, K. A., de Niet, G. J., Knipscheer, J. W., Kleber, R. J., & Hutschemaekers, G. J. M. (2015). The effectiveness of art therapy in the treatment of traumatized adults: A systematic review on art therapy and trauma. *Trauma, Violence, and Abuse, 16*(2), 220–228. https://doi.org/10.1177/1524838014555032

Sholt, M., & Gavron, T. (2006). Therapeutic qualities of clay-work in art therapy and psychotherapy: A review. *Art Therapy: Journal of the American Art Therapy Association, 23*(2), 66–72.

Skop, M., Darewych, O. H., Root, J., & Mason, J. (2022). Exploring intimate partner violence survivors' experiences with group art therapy. *International Journal of Art Therapy, 27*(4), 159–168. https://doi.org/10.1080/17454832.2022.2124298

Spiegel, D., Malchiodi, C., Backos, A., & Collie, K. (2006). Art therapy for combat-related PTSD: Recommendations for research and practice. *Art Therapy, 23*(4), 157–164.

Steele, W., & Malchiodi, C. A. (2012). *Trauma-informed practices with children and adolescents.* Routledge/Taylor & Francis Group.

Stinley, N. E., Norris, D. O., & Hinds, P. S. (2015). Creating mandalas for the management of acute pain symptoms in pediatric patients. *Art Therapy, 32*(2), 46–53. https://doi.org/10.1080/07421656.2015.1028871

Wessells, M. G., & Kostelny, K. (2022). The psychosocial impacts of intimate partner violence against women in LMIC contexts: Toward a holistic approach. *International Journal of Environmental Research and Public Health, 19*(21), 14488. https://doi.org/10.3390/ijerph192114488

World Health Organization. (n.d.). *Intimate partner violence.* https://apps.who.int/violence-info/intimate-partner-violence

World Health Organization (WHO). (2021). *Violence against women prevalence estimates, 2018.* https://www.who.int/publications/i/item/9789240026681

Zhang, X., Wen, K., Ding, H., & Zhou, X. (2024). Experiencing art creation as a therapeutic intervention to relieve anxiety—a case study of a university's ceramic art course. *Frontiers in Psychiatry, 15,* 1334240. https://doi.org/10.3389/fpsyt.2024.1334240

IMAGE CREDITS

Fig. 8.1: Generated using ChatGPT.

Fig. 8.2: Generated using ChatGPT.

Fig. 8.3: Generated using ChatGPT.

Fig. 8.4: Generated using ChatGPT.

PART IV

Moving Forward

CHAPTER 9

Emerging Trends in Art Therapy for PTSD

Art therapy is an evolving field which holds promise for the treatment of post-traumatic stress disorder (PTSD). Its capacity to provide alternative avenues for expression and healing makes it a valuable complement to traditional therapeutic modalities.

The current chapter explores the emerging trends and future directions in art therapy for the treatment of PTSD, including the integration of art therapy with traditional modalities of treatment, the impact of technological advancements, and the expansion of supportive research. Upon completion of this chapter, readers will be able to:

1. Explain how art therapy may be used in conjunction with cognitive processing therapy (CPT), eye movement desensitization and reprocessing (EMDR), and narrative therapies (NT);
2. Describe the potential benefits and downsides to the inclusion of digital art in art therapy; and
3. Provide an overview of the nature and limitations of current research in art therapy effectiveness research.

Integration of Art Therapy with Established PTSD Treatments

According to the *Clinical Practice Guideline for the Treatment of PTSD* (APA, 2017) and the National Institute for Health and Care Excellence guideline (2018), CPT, EMDR, and NT are the treatments of choice for PTSD. While evidence supports the effectiveness of these approaches, it also highlights the fact that more than one-third of patients, especially those with poor verbal memory or difficulties with talking about their traumatic experiences, do not benefit from these interventions (Bradley et al., 2005).

Art therapy is increasingly recognized as a valuable complement to other therapeutic modalities for treating PTSD (Campbell et al., 2016; Heijman et al., 2024). The Department of Veteran Affairs (VA), for example, has employed art therapists since 1980 and continues to use art therapy to help veterans with PTSD cope with their symptoms (American Art Therapy Association, n.d.).

When considering the future of art therapy, we will likely see its increased utilization as a valued complement to more traditional therapies and establish itself as a stand-alone mode of treatment.

Art Therapy and Cognitive Processing Therapy

Cognitive processing therapy (CPT) is a specific type of cognitive therapy designed to challenge the distorted and negative cognitions associated with trauma (Forbes et al., 2012). While identifying and challenging the client's distorted beliefs often takes the form of written or verbal disclosure, engaging in the creative activities of art therapy provides an additional medium for identifying and challenging the client's interpretations and beliefs. This combination allows for a more comprehensive processing of traumatic experiences, engaging multiple areas of the brain and facilitating healing.

In practice, integrating art therapy into CPT can facilitate the identification, challenging, and reframing of negative, dysfunctional thoughts. For example, clients can create visual representations of their traumatic experiences, which are then used as focal points during CPT sessions to challenge maladaptive beliefs. In this situation, construction of a cohesive visual trauma narrative may help clients transform, reinterpret, and reintegrate dissociated sensory memories into explicit memory (Campbell et al., 2016). Decker and associates (2018) describe a randomized, controlled trial supporting the value of art therapy interventions when complementing cognitive processing therapy. One of the art-based interventions employed by these researchers was the creation of a six-image visual trauma narrative reflecting (1) time before the trauma, (2) an image of the last moment the client recalled before the trauma occurred, (3) an image of what happened during the traumatic event, (4) an image of the moment immediately after the trauma, (5) an image of a time when the client was safe from the physical threats of trauma, and (6) a time when the client tried to self-soothe. These images were posted and used to assist the client in narrating the traumatic event from a third-person perspective, thus facilitating a reprocessing and reintegration of the events.

Veterans who have experienced art therapy in conjunction with CPT have noted that it has helped them gain healthy distancing from the painful memories thus enhancing trauma recall and access to their emotions (Campbell et al., 2016). Given this value of artwork in facilitating trauma recall and trauma processing, it is likely that the future will provide more evidence of its effectiveness as a supplemental intervention to cognitive processing therapy.

Eye Movement Desensitization and Reprocessing (EMDR)

EMDR is an evidence-based psychotherapy that facilitates the processing of traumatic memories (Valiente-Gómez et al., 2017). Art therapy strategies can be used along with EMDR to help clients visually represent a safe place, perhaps by using collage materials and as grounding before processing traumatic memories. The use of sequential art, such as creating a storyboard, can help clients externalize and organize traumatic memories, facilitating their processing during EMDR.

However, perhaps the primary value of employing art therapy with EMDR is in the promotion of bilateral stimulation, which is believed to be the center of the effectiveness of EMDR. The Adaptive Information Processing (AIP) model (Hill, 2020), which serves as the rationale for EMDR, posits that bilateral stimulation permits the complete processing of traumatic memories, reducing trauma symptoms. EMDR therapy taps into this bilateral stimulation by systematically engaging a client's eye movement (Malhotra et al., 2024; Shapiro & Forrest, 2016). Bilateral drawing (Tripp, 2023) also engages interhemispheric activity and, as a result, promotes adaptive information processing. Several authors have proposed art therapy approaches that engage bilateral stimulation to integrate traumatic memories (e.g., Brown, 2010; Malchiodi, 2020; Talwar, 2007).

Bilateral drawing involves spontaneously engaging both hands in drawing with chalks, pastels, or other easily manipulated art materials. The focus is on bilateral stimulation rather than creating a specific image (Malchiodi, 2020).

Art therapy can serve as bilateral stimulation, engaging both brain hemispheres and facilitating a client's externalization of memories, making them more accessible for verbal processing (Malchiodi, 2020). For example, Talwar (2007) asked her client to get up physically and, while concentrating on a traumatic memory, paint alternating between dominant and nondominant hands. She found that this process facilitated the client's sensory awareness and promoted emotional regulation. Research (e.g., Tripp, 2007) demonstrating the value of including art therapy interventions with EDMR will serve as a springboard for future consideration of this integrated approach to treating PTSD, especially for those clients for whom verbal recall and disclosure of traumatic memories is challenged.

Narrative Therapy

Narrative therapy (White & Epston, 1990) is grounded in the belief that individuals construct meaning through stories and that these narratives shape their identities and experiences. Narrative therapy assists clients to externalize their problems by separating the traumatic experience from the person. This allows the person to see themselves as the story's author and empowers them to find the illogic and holes in the story, deconstruct it, and reconstruct a more accurate and functional narrative. By reconstructing trauma narratives, individuals can gain a sense of agency and coherence, which is often disrupted by traumatic events (White & Epston, 1990).

Art therapy can enrich narrative approaches by providing a medium for externalizing the experience, thus facilitating the retrieval and expression of implicit memories. The tangible representation of the client's memories and internal experiences not only helps externalize the narrative but also provides distance between the narrative and the client (Campbell et al., 2016).

Clients can create a series of artworks depicting significant life events, including traumatic experiences, and written narratives that chronicle their life stories. The use of artwork enables clients to externalize and organize their narratives. It provides the psychological distance necessary to process and reconstruct the narrative. And the artwork can serve as a focal point for therapeutic discussion and the integration of the traumatic memory into the client's autobiographical narrative (Heijman et al., 2024).

Integrating art therapy interventions with narrative therapy is effective. Given the value added by artwork to narrative therapy, it can be expected that the future will see expanded employment of art with narrative therapy in the future and research to support its effectiveness.

The Emergence of Digital Art in Art Therapy

Art therapy often involves tangible mediums such as painting, drawing, and sculpture. However, digital art has become a significant tool in this therapeutic landscape.

Digital art therapy combines principles of traditional art therapy with digital media, allowing clients to create and manipulate images using technology. Digital tools such as tablets, styluses, and specialized software have expanded the possibilities for creative expression in therapy. These tools not only provide a mess-free and accessible medium for clients but also offer unique features that can be particularly empowering for clients, particularly for those with disabilities or sensory sensitivities (Donnari et al., 2019).

Digital tools offer unique features, including the ability to undo actions, experiment with various textures and colors without material constraints, and easily store and share artwork. Such capabilities can enhance the therapeutic process by providing clients with a flexible and nonpermanent medium to explore their emotions and experiences.

Digital art allows for the documentation of the creative process, enabling clients and therapists to review and reflect on the evolution of artwork over time. Moreover, using digital media can facilitate the employment of art therapy through online delivery (Zubala et al., 2021).

Studies have demonstrated that digital art therapy can effectively alleviate symptoms of anxiety, depression, and trauma, offering a viable alternative to traditional methods (Zubala et al., 2021). Additionally, clients have reported experiencing stress relief and improved emotional regulation through creative digital expression, underscoring the therapeutic value of digital art interventions (Zubala et al., 2021).

The use of digital art is not without its critics. A primary focus of concern highlights the value of tactile engagement with the art materials as invaluable for assisting clients in expressing and processing emotions and the concern that digital art limits this critical aspect of art therapy (Klorer, 2009). The reality, however, is that digital technology will be a permanent fixture in our lives, including art therapy. Studies exploring client experiences with digital art therapy, the effectiveness of various digital tools, and the development of best practice guidelines are essential and hopefully will be addressed in the near future (Kaimal et al., 2016). With emerging research supporting the effectiveness of digital tools in art therapy, we are likely to see an expansion of their use in the treatment of PTSD.

Advances in Neurobiological Understanding

Another trend shaping the future of art therapy for the treatment of PTSD is the growing body of research (e.g., Barnett & Vasiu, 2024) that links creative expression with neurobiological healing. Studies (e.g., Walker et al., 2018) using functional MRI (fMRI) and electroencephalography (EEG) have shown that art therapy can stimulate brain regions involved in emotional regulation, memory processing, and stress reduction.

Creating art has been found to activate the prefrontal cortex, helping individuals gain better control over intrusive thoughts and emotional dysregulation. Additionally, engaging in visual art can reduce activity in the amygdala, the brain's fear center, thereby diminishing the fight-or-flight response associated with PTSD (Shin et al., 2006).

These findings have strengthened the scientific credibility of art therapy. It is this type of validation that will encourage its expanded utilization in the treatment of PTSD.

Effectiveness

The American Psychological Association developed a policy on the evidence-based practice (EBP) of psychotherapy (APA Presidential Task Force on Evidence-Based Practice, 2006) that emphasizes integrating the best-available research from meta-analyses, randomized controlled trials, effectiveness studies, and process studies as well as information obtained from single-case reports, systematic case studies, qualitative and ethnographic research, and clinical observation. Despite decades of use and demonstrated positive impacts on specific outcome measures (Dunphy et al., 2019; Kaimal et al., 2016), acceptance and implementation of art therapy as a stand-alone or even supplemental treatment for PTSD is hindered by the lack of rigorous, large randomized controlled research. Maddox and associates (2024), for example, found only 21 of 868 studies that were randomized controlled trials.

Research on the effectiveness of art therapy in the treatment of PTSD has been primarily qualitative, reporting on case studies or small N outcomes (e.g., Maddox et al., 2024; Schouten et al., 2015). Small sample sizes and inconsistent treatment protocols make it difficult to draw reliable conclusions about art therapy's efficacy.

The advancement of art therapy as an evidence-based approach to the treatment of PTSD will require more robust research. Future research will need to offer data from studies using larger sample sizes, standardized protocols, and randomized controlled designs if art therapy is to be fully embraced as a treatment for PTSD.

From Knowledge to Application

Digital tools such as tablets, styluses, and specialized software have expanded the possibilities for creative expression in therapy. However, the often-raised criticism of using digital art tools in therapy is that they lack the tactile element essential to expressing and processing emotions. Exercise 9.1 invites you to experience digital versus tangible mediums in coloring a mandala.

EXERCISE 9.1 Coloring Mandala

Directions. This exercise invites you to contrast the experience of coloring mandalas online versus using tangible materials.

Step 1: Go to one of the sites listed below, select a mandala and print a copy.

MandalaMaker.online: https://mandalamaker.online/coloring-online/#google_vignette

ColoringBook: https://coloringbook.pics/antistress-coloring-pages/mandala-57/#google_vignett

Step 2:

a. Using colored pencils, markers, or crayons, color your mandala.

b. Using the same mandala, color your mandala online using the digital coloring tools. You can use the same colors as in your tangible creation or choose others.

Step 3: Process your experience with an eye to the therapeutic effect of coloring each mandala.

a. Describe the physical or emotional pluses and minuses you experienced when employing digital tools.

b. Describe the physical or emotional pluses and minuses you experienced when employing a tangible medium.

c. Using a scale of 1 = *very little* to 10 = *extremely so*, use the table to assess your experience with each of these mediums.

	Tangible Medium	Digital Tool
The degree to which you were engaged and interested.		
The level of calm (emotional) that you experienced.		
The level of physical relaxation that you experienced.		
The degree to which any worrisome or concerning thoughts were blocked or disengaged.		
Your willingness to employ as a therapeutic intervention for clients who are anxious, stressed, or traumatized.		

The Takeaway

Art therapy continues to evolve as a complementary and potentially stand-alone treatment for PTSD. The integration of art therapy with traditional PTSD treatments, advancements in digital art, and the push for stronger research methodologies mark significant trends in the field. As ongoing studies expand the evidence base, art therapy will likely gain greater recognition and implementation within trauma treatment frameworks.

Keystones

- Art therapy is increasingly used alongside cognitive processing therapy (CPT), eye movement desensitization and reprocessing (EMDR), and narrative therapy (NT) to enhance treatment outcomes, particularly for individuals who struggle with verbalizing their trauma.
- Art therapy helps clients externalize and visually process distorted trauma-related beliefs, supporting cognitive restructuring through structured visual narratives.
- Art therapy enhances EMDR through bilateral stimulation techniques like bilateral drawing, helping clients process and integrate traumatic memories.
- By creating visual narratives, clients can organize and reframe their trauma experiences, improving emotional resilience and memory integration.
- Digital tools expand access to art therapy, allowing clients to engage with therapy innovatively. They also address physical limitations and increase accessibility through online platforms.

- By leveraging the creative process, art therapy facilitates the expression and integration of traumatic experiences, leading to neurobiological changes that underpin symptom reduction.
- Limited large-scale, randomized controlled trials hinder the widespread acceptance of art therapy as a validated PTSD treatment. More rigorous research with standardized protocols is necessary.
- As research expands, art therapy is expected to gain increased recognition as a complementary and potentially stand-alone PTSD treatment.

ADDITIONAL RESOURCES

Crowther, P. (2022). *Digital art, aesthetic creation: The birth of a medium*. Routledge.

Davis, E., Fitzgerald, J., Jacobs, S., & Marchand, J. (Eds.) (2023). *EMDR and creative arts therapies*. Routledge.

Malchiodi, C.A (Ed.) (2018). *The handbook of art therapy and digital technology*. Jessica Kingsley Publishers.

REFERENCES

American Art Therapy Association (n.d.). *Art therapy, posttraumatic stress disorder, and veterans*. American Art Therapy Association. https://www.americansforthearts.org/sites/default/files/RMveteransPTSD.pdf

American Psychological Association. (2017). *Clinical practice guideline for the treatment of posttraumatic stress disorder (PTSD) in adults*. American Psychological Association. https://www.apa.org/ptsd-guideline

APA Presidential Task Force on Evidence-Based Practice. (2006). Evidence-based practice in psychology. *American Psychologist, 61*(4), 271–285.

Barnett, K. S., & Vasiu, F. (2024). How the arts heal: A review of the neural mechanisms behind the therapeutic effects of creative arts on mental and physical health. *Frontiers in Behavioral Neuroscience, 18*, 1422361. https://doi.org/10.3389/fnbeh.2024.1422361

Bradley, R., Greene, J., Russ, E., Dutra, L., & Westen, D. (2005). A multidimensional meta-analysis of psychotherapy for PTSD. *American Journal of Psychiatry, 162*(2), 214–227.

Brown, L. E. (2010). Developing a short-term art therapy protocol for a university counseling center to address trauma.

Campbell, M., Decker, K. P., Kruk, K., & Deaver, S. P. (2016). Art therapy and cognitive processing therapy for combat-related PTSD: A randomized controlled trial. *Art Therapy: Journal of the American Art Therapy Association*, 33(4), 169–177. https://doi.org/10.1080/07421656.2016.1226643

Decker, K. P., Deaver, S. P., Abbey, V., Campbell, M., & Turpin, C. (2018). Quantitatively improved treatment outcomes for combat-associated PTSD with adjunctive art therapy: Randomized controlled trial. *Art Therapy*, 35(4), 184–194. https://doi.org/10.1080/07421656.2018.1540822

Donnari, S., Canonico, V., Fatuzzo, G., Bedetti, C., Marchiafava, M., Menna, M., & Elisei, S. (2019). New technologies for art therapy interventions tailored to severe disabilities. *Psychiatria Danubina, 31*(Suppl 3), 462–466.

Dunphy, K., Baker, F. A., Dumaresq, E., Carroll-Haskins, K., Eickholt, J., Ercole, M., Kaimal, G., Meyer, K., Sajnani, N., Shamir, O. Y., & Wosch, T. (2019). Creative arts interventions to address depression in older adults: A systematic review of outcomes, processes, and mechanisms. *Frontiers in Psychology, 9*, 2655. https://doi.org/10.3389/fpsyg.2018.02655

Forbes, D., Lloyd, D., Nixon, R. D. V., Elliott, P., Varker, T., Perry, D., Bryant, R. A., & Creamer, M. (2012). A multisite randomized controlled effectiveness trial of cognitive processing therapy for military-related posttraumatic stress disorder. *Journal of Anxiety Disorders, 26*(3), 442–452.

Heijman, J., Wouters, H., Schouten, K. A., & Haeyen, S. (2024). Effectiveness of trauma-focused art therapy (TFAT) for psychological trauma: Study protocol of a multiple-baseline single-case experimental design. *BMJ Open, 14*(1), e081917. https://doi.org/10.1136/bmjopen-2023-081917

Hill, M. D. (2020). Adaptive Information Processing theory: Origins, principles, applications, and evidence. *Journal of Evidence-based Social Work, 17*(3), 317–331. https://doi.org/10.1080/26408066.2020.1748155

Kaimal, G., Rattigan, M., Miller, G., & Haddy, J. (2016). Implications of national trends in digital media use for art therapy practice. *Journal of Clinical Art Therapy, 3*(1), 6.

Klorer, P. G. (2009). The effects of technological overload on children: An art therapist's perspective. *Art Therapy, 26*(2), 80–82.

Malchiodi, C. A. (2020). *Trauma and expressive arts therapy: Brain, body, and imagination in the healing process.* Guilford Press.

Maddox, G. A., Bodner, G. E., Christian, M. W., & Williamson, P. (2024). On the effectiveness of visual arts therapy for traumatic experiences: A systematic review and meta-analysis. *Clinical Psychology & Psychotherapy, 31*(4), e3041. https://doi.org/10.1002/cpp.3041

Malhotra, B., Jones, L. C., Spooner, H., Levy, C., Kaimal, G., & Williamson, J. B. (2024). A conceptual framework for a neurophysiological basis of art therapy for PTSD. *Frontiers in Human Neuroscience, 18*, 1351757.

National Institute for Health and Care Excellence. (2018). *Post-traumatic stress disorder NICE guideline (NG116).* National Institute for Health and Care Excellence. https://www.nice.org.uk/guidance/ng116

Schouten, K. A., de Niet, G. J., Knipscheer, J. W., Kleber, R. J., & Hutschemaekers, G. J. M. (2015). The effectiveness of art therapy in treating traumatized adults: A systematic review on art therapy and trauma. *Trauma, Violence, & Abuse, 16*(2), 220–228. https://doi.org/10.1177/1524838014555032

Shapiro, F., & Forrest, M. S. (2016). *EMDR: The breakthrough therapy for overcoming anxiety, stress, and trauma.* Hachette.

Shin, L. M., Rauch, S. L., & Pitman, R. K. (2006). Amygdala, medial prefrontal cortex, and hippocampal function in PTSD. *Annals of the New York Academy of Sciences, 1071*(1), 67–79. https://doi.org/10.1196/annals.1364.007

Talwar, S. (2007). Accessing traumatic memory through art making: An art therapy trauma protocol (ATTP). *The Arts in Psychotherapy, 34*(1), 22–35. https://doi.org/10.1016/j.aip.2006.09.001

Tripp, T. (2007). A short-term therapy approach to processing trauma: Art therapy and bilateral stimulation. *Art Therapy, 24*(4), 176–183.

Tripp, T. (2023). Art therapy and EMDR: Integrating cognitive, somatic, and emotional processing for treating trauma. In E. Davis, J. Fitzgerald, S. Jacobs, & J. Marchand (Eds.), *EMDR and creative arts therapies* (pp. 176–207). Routledge.

Valiente-Gómez, A., Moreno-Alcázar, A., Treen, D., Cedrón, C., Colom, F., Pérez, V., & Amann, B. L. (2017). EMDR beyond PTSD: A systematic literature review. *Frontiers in Psychology, 8*, 1668. https://doi.org/10.3389/fpsyg.2017.01668

Walker, M. S., Stamper, A. M., Nathan, D. E., & Riedy, G. (2018). Art therapy and underlying fMRI brain patterns in military TBI: A case series. *International Journal of Art Therapy, 23*(4), 180–187. DOI: 10.1080/17454832.2018.1473453

White, M., & Epston, D. (1990). *Narrative means to therapeutic ends.* W.W. Norton.

Zubala, A., Kennell, N., & Hackett, S. (2021). Art therapy in the digital world: An integrative review of current practice and future directions. *Frontiers in Psychology, 12*, 595536. https://doi.org/10.3389/fpsyg.2021.600070

CHAPTER 10

Ethical Considerations

Art therapists are guided in their practice decisions by core values of (1) autonomy, respecting the rights of clients to make informed choices; (2) justice, committing to treating all persons with fairness; (3) fidelity, acting with honesty and integrity; (4) creativity, cultivating imagination for furthering understanding of self, others, and the world; (5) nonmaleficence, striving to conduct themselves and their practice in a way that causes no harm, and (6) beneficence, promoting well-being and enhancing the welfare of others (AATA, 2013). Except for creativity, these core values are espoused by other human service provider associations, including the American Counseling Association (2014) and the American Psychological Association (2017).

As a distinct mental health profession and practice, art therapists and those using art as a meta-verbal intervention within their practice find that the manifestation of these values within their practice is often confronted by unique ethical challenges presented by the employment of art as a therapeutic intervention. The current chapter reviews the unique ethical considerations guiding the implementation of art therapy in the treatment of clients presenting with trauma and PTSD. Upon completion of this chapter, readers will be able to:

1. Identify core ethical considerations unique to the practice of art therapy vis-à-vis more traditional forms of mental service provision;
2. Explain the unique factors to be considered by art therapists in their collection and maintenance of clinical notes;
3. Describe the minimum entry requirements into the profession of art therapy; and
4. Identify advanced certification opportunities for those in the field of art therapy.

Competency: The Fundamental Ethical Consideration

A fundamental ethical principle guiding all mental health practitioners is to provide only the services for which they have been trained, supervised, and demonstrated competency. The *Code governing Standard of Practice, Eligility for and Regulation of Credentials, and Discplinary Procedures* (ATCB, 2024) directs art therapists not to "engage in therapy practices or procedures that are beyond their scope of practice, experience, training, and education" (Principle 1.1.6).

To this end, the American Art Therapy Association (https://arttherapy.org/becoming-art-therapist/) has identified the entry-level educational requirements for art therapists and the path to advanced credentials and certifications.

Entry-Level

As the AATA (2022) describes, art therapists must obtain a master's degree for entry-level practice and possess a strong foundation in psychological theories, counseling techniques, and mental health interventions.

The AATA (2022) calls for graduate-level coursework in the following areas: the creative process, developmental psychology, abnormal psychology, group therapy, art therapy assessment, psychodiagnostics, research methods, and multicultural competency development and cultural humility. In addition to the course work in psychology, those seeking entrance into the field as art therapists must have training in two- and three-dimensional art media and processes (e.g., painting, clay work, digital art). Finally, students seeking to enter the field of art therapy must also complete, at minimum, 100 hours of supervised practicum and 600 hours of supervised art therapy clinical internship.

Certifications

The Art Therapy Credentials Board (ATCB; https://atcb.org) is independent of the American Art Therapy Association, and it oversees and administers advanced certifications and credentials. Credentialing and certification are offered through the ATCB (Art Therapy Credentials Board, 2024).

As a nationally certifying body, the ATCB administers the following certifications:

Provisional registered art therapist (ATR-P) for individuals who have completed their degree and are engaged in a supervisory relationship with a qualified supervisor(s);

Registered art therapist (ATR) for those individuals who meet established standards, with successful completion of advanced specific graduate-level education in art therapy and supervised, post-graduate art therapy experience and;

Board certification (ATR-BC) for individuals who complete the highest-level art therapy credential by passing a national examination and demonstrating comprehensive knowledge of the theories and clinical skills used in art therapy.

Given the ever-evolving nature of art therapy, competency does not end with acquiring a degree or certification. The American Art Therapy Association (2013) directs its members to "keep informed of developments in their field through educational activities and clinical experiences" (AATA, 2013; Principle 6.1). Members are also reminded to "refrain from using art materials, creative processes, equipment, technology or therapy practices that are beyond their scope of practice, experience, training and education (AATA, 2013; Principle 6.2).

Competency with Diverse Client Populations and Cultural Sensitivity

As with other mental health providers, art therapists are called to be sensitive to the specific influence of their clients' race, ethnicity, culture, nationality, gender, religion, socioeconomic status, political views, sexual orientation, geographic region, physical capacity or disability, and historical or current experiences with the dominant culture and recognize how these factors influence the expression and interpretation of art (AATA, 2011). To this end the AATA directs members to "take reasonable steps to ensure that they are sensitive to difference that exist among cultures" (AATA, 2013; Principle 7.2).

Art therapists must have the ability to understand, appreciate, and effectively work with individuals from diverse cultural backgrounds. Art therapists must be aware of their own values, beliefs, and how these may affect cross-cultural therapy interventions (AATA, 2013; Principle 7.3).

When working with clients from diverse backgrounds, the art therapist should use materials, images, and symbols that resonate with the client's cultural identity. Therapists must also know the cultural meanings associated with certain symbols, colors, and artistic expressions and avoid cultural appropriation in artistic interventions (see Case Illustration 10.1).

CASE ILLUSTRATION 10.1 Cultural Appropriation in Art Therapy

Daniel, a 16-year-old Navajo (Diné) teenager, had recently moved, along with his parents, from his reservation to an urban area. Daniel's parents brought him to therapy because of his expression of feeling depressed and alone. Daniel shared that he felt disconnected from his friends and his cultural roots.

The non-Native therapist had recently developed an interest and some initial training in using art as therapeutic intervention. The therapist decided to incorporate an art exercise, one that was "culturally relevant" in his work with Daniel. The hope was that selecting the right materials or assigning a culturally meaningful exercise would help strengthen the working alliance with Daniel.

During the second session, the therapist presented Daniel with a tray and colored sand and invited him to create a design representing his feelings. Daniel began engaging with the material, but he soon grew tense and withdrew from the task. When asked why he stopped, Daniel explained that he did not think he "should be doing this" and abruptly swept away the sand in the design he had just begun to create.

Seeing the reaction, the therapist gently and empathetically invited Daniel to share his feelings and reactions. Daniel explained:

> The Shaman of my tribe would "paint" by letting colored sand fall carefully through his fingers. It would create holy, healing symbols. The paintings are believed to be dynamic, living, sacred entities that could transform an ailing person's mental and physical state. I'm not a Shaman and I shouldn't be doing this.

While the therapist in Case Illustration 10.1 had good intentions, using a sacred art form outside its proper context was counterproductive and alienated his client. Art therapists need both cultural awareness and cultural humility, which will allow them to be open to being educated by the client on symbolism in the artwork that has specific significance within their culture, which may have been unfamiliar to the therapist. Thus, rather than assuming what is "healing" for a client, therapists should provide space for clients to guide how their culture informs their self-expression. Understanding a client's cultural background is essential to providing effective interventions (AATA, 2013).

Nonmaleficence: Do No Harm

Art therapy can evoke deep emotions and unlock unconscious memories. The images, materials, or techniques employed may inadvertently evoke a client's traumatic memories that surface unexpectedly during the creative process, leading clients to experience intense emotional or physiological distress. It is possible that the materials selected or the activity employed can result in retraumatization. Experiencing retraumatization can severely undermine the therapeutic process, eroding the client's trust in the therapist and, by extension, in therapy itself.

Art therapists are guided by the value of nonmaleficence, or "do no harm" (AATA, 2013), and seek to balance creative expression with emotional safety. While creating a safe therapeutic environment is an aspiration for all therapeutic modalities, employing art as an intervention in trauma-informed care requires additional consideration of elements that may undermine that safety. The tasks and materials must allow for expressive freedom while ensuring emotional safety. Therapists must balance structuring and directing an activity and giving clients control over their creative process.

Given the need to allow for creativity and structure for emotional safety, therapists should discuss with their clients specific art elements or assignments that may elicit distressing memories. In this way, clients are empowered to modify their approach or even their choice of materials to reduce the possibility of retraumatization. In situations where intense emotions are aroused, therapists can assist clients with grounding exercises to help them reorient to the present moment and prevent them from becoming too overwhelmed by past emotions. When it is clear that the client is struggling with anxiety or feeling overwhelmed with the intervention being employed, art therapists may stop the process and invite the client to engage in activities known to have a grounding, calming effect such as coloring mandalas or making collages, but with positive imagery or, as presented in Case Illustration 10.2, engaging in repetitive pattern activities like dotting (i.e., repetitive, rhythmic act of creating patterns with dots).

CASE ILLUSTRATION 10.2 **Dotting: A Calming Activity**

Jamal, a nine-year-old, had been seeing Dr. K. for the past six months in response to the trauma incurred after observing his baby sister drown in the family pool. Jamal has been very engaging in therapy, but on this particular day, the anniversary of the incident, he was clearly upset and too overwhelmed to engage in his clay work or to sit and talk with Dr. K.

Fifteen minutes into the session, when it was clear that Jamal's anxiety was interfering with their previous approach to therapy, Dr. K. stopped the session and said:

> I have an idea. Let's do something different today. Rather than working with the clay, unless that is what you want to do, how about if we do some dotting?

Jamal, while attentive, was clearly confused by the word *dotting*. Dr. K. selected a bright blue marker and began to repetitively and rhythmically make dots on a white sheet of paper.

> It's simple—you pick a color or several color markers and you can either try to make a design with your dots or go where your dots take you. In fact, you can do it with your eyes open or closed, or alternate doing both." (Dr. K. demonstrated.)

After marking the page, Dr. K. stopped and asked Jamal, "Do you see any design or anything that looks familiar?" Jamal looked over the page and, after reflecting for a minute, excitedly pointed to the upper right corner and said these all look like "smiley faces, overlapping each other."

For the next five minutes, Jamal placed random dots across the page. He exchanged his color pencils three times and even began dotting the page with his eyes closed. He became absorbed in the repetitive, rhythmic activity.

His upset and anxiety were replaced by a focused calm. As he and Dr. K. finished searching the dots for familiar images, Dr. K. asked, "How did that make you feel?" Jamal responded: "It was fun. It kind of helped my brain slow down."

The rhythmic, repetitive nature of dotting provided Jamal with a nonverbal, sensory-based way to self-soothe. It also allowed Jamal and Dr. K. to return to their clay tray and continue with the session.

Informed Consent

As mental health professionals, art therapists are directed to provide clients with all the relevant information about the processes to be employed and the potential risks and benefits of art therapy so that clients can make an informed decision regarding their desire to pursue therapy. Art therapists should gather signed consent forms that verify clients' understanding of the nature of art therapy and the risks, expectations, and benefits.

In addition to the traditional areas and content covered in informed consent, art therapists must inform clients of the possible emotional and psychological reactions that can be elicited by using the materials to create art. Clients also need information regarding their artwork's specific use, maintenance, and storage (Atkins, 2007). The AATA (2013) directs its members to:

> explain how client artwork will be stored while the client is receiving art therapy services and the duration of retention for the actual artwork, photographs or digital images. (AATA, 2013; Principle 4.7)

It is important to remember that the client has the right to control access to their artwork. As such, updating signed informed consent forms across sessions is fundamental to ethical art therapy practices. Continuous dialogue about consent throughout the therapeutic process reinforces client autonomy and empowerment (Zawadi, 2024).

A template for an art therapy informed consent form can be found at https://www.jotform.com/form-templates/art-therapy-informed-consent-form, and an example of one used by board-certified art therapist Melinda Kostecky can be found at https://sophia.center/wp-content/uploads/2023/02/Art-Therapy-Consent-for-Treatment_FillableFields_Feb23.pdf.

Clinical Notes/Privacy

Taking and maintaining clinical therapy notes is essential to developing and adjusting treatment plans, tracking client progress, communicating effectively with others, and managing risk. In addition to its practical value, taking and maintaining clinical notes is an ethical and, in some states, a legal mandate (APA, 2007). Like other healthcare professionals, art therapists must create and maintain clinical records but given the nature of their records, this can become cumbersome.

Moon (2000) suggests that the art therapy progress notes should include: identifying information on the patient; the session date and duration; a description of what the patient did during the session; the art materials used and the images created; a summary of things the patient said; specific quotes from the session if relevant; a reference to the current treatment goals and actions the art therapist took in addressing them; and a summary of the session. These elements are integral to the nature and outcome of art therapy and must be reflected in the clinical notes (Morgan, 2023). Some (e.g., Hammond & Gantt, 1998) have suggested that while an art therapist may provide an elaborate and expansive description of clients' art, the clinical value may be better served with the inclusion of the actual art product, or a picture of that artwork.

Inclusion of the art product, or a photograph of it, presents several challenges, including (a) what to include in the notes, (b) the issue of interpretation, and (c) how to store and maintain the privacy of these notes when they include art products.

A Model for Inclusion

Hauck et al. (2025) have proposed a documentation model that can guide art therapists in collecting and maintaining clinical records. These authors suggest the following elements to guide decisions around clinical note-taking.

1. **D**escribe the art piece(s) without interpretation, describing colors, size, medium, element arrangement, depiction, written words, characters, and symbols.
2. **R**eview the client's approach and process of art-making, identifying materials offered and those selected.
3. **A**ssess the meaning of the work and process using client input and interpretation.
4. Consider **W**hat Else is significant and should be included. Therapists may find a client's sensory reaction to materials or tasks of clinical significance, or perhaps something relevant happened during the art-making activity that should be noted.
5. Write a **S**ummary that gives an overall view of the session.

Interpretation

Artwork is nonliteral and has no automatic, fixed meaning (Morgan, 2023). When including a client's artwork within the clinical file, the therapist should provide a verbal explanation or description. However, interpreting or assigning meaning to the client's work is highly subjective and should be employed judiciously (Coles, 2018).

When creating notes, art therapists need to identify what reflects their impressions, their interpretation distinguishing this information from a more "objective" description of the what, where, and why of the artwork. It is also valuable to include client commentary about the process, the product, and its meaning.

Storage and Confidentiality

Securing clinical notes and client information is central to all mental health therapeutic practice. Professional organizations provide practice guidelines for storage and release of clinical notes. These guidelines reflect the profession's unique code of ethics and adhere to local, state, and federal law.

Therapists are ethically obligated to safeguard clients' privacy by securing all testing data and clinical and progress notes. For an art therapist, the data collected and maintained can be somewhat expansive and even cumbersome, assuming clients' actual artwork is included. The American Art Therapy Association (AATA) emphasizes that art therapists must treat clients' artworks with the same level of confidentiality as verbal disclosures.

> Art therapists regard client artwork as protected information and the client's property. In some practice settings, client artwork or artwork representations may be considered part of the clinical record retained by the therapist and/or agency for a reasonable amount of time consistent with state regulations and sound clinical practice. (AATA, 2013; Principle 4.0)

While confidentiality is paramount in art therapy, it can be somewhat challenging to maintain since it extends to the physical artworks clients create. Including a client's artwork in the official file flows from the position that the client's creations are central to the therapeutic process, serving as tangible reflections of their inner experiences and providing evidence of progress, should such be noted. While clearly of value, this inclusion poses a challenge for safety and storage.

Given space limitations, it can safely be assumed that storing large amounts of client artwork for long periods is simply untenable. When considering which pieces to maintain, therapists may want to consider the following:

1. What information would help support their clinical decisions if challenged by a board complaint or a malpractice allegation?
2. Which piece(s) supports the therapist's diagnosis and treatment choice and provides evidence of progress?
3. What information would be helpful to any subsequent art therapist treating the client, especially in the case of continuity of care?

Storage can remain a challenge even when the therapist is being somewhat selective in which pieces to include in the client's file. It has been suggested that a photograph can be used as a substitute record for the actual creation (ATCB, 2024, Principle 2.1.9).

When using photographs, the therapist may find it helpful to include a piece of paper as part of the photo showing the date of the session and the client's initials (Atkins, 2007). These act as verification of the authenticity of the item and its place within the therapeutic journey.

From Knowledge to Application

Understanding, embracing, and applying the ethics and standards of the helping profession are essential for all who enter it. When employing art therapy as a stand-alone approach to treatment or as a supplementary form of therapy, the therapist must be able to respond to the unique ethical challenges presented by this mode of treatment.

Exercise 10.1 invites you to consider ethical challenges unique to art therapy and decide on an ethical response.

EXERCISE 10.1 **Reflect—Discuss—Decide**

Directions: Ethical challenges are rarely clear-cut. The following are scenarios in which an ethical practice decision is required. With classmates or colleagues, review each scenario, reflect, discuss, and decide on a path.

Confidentiality and Mandated Reporting

- You are working with a teenage client who shares his artwork with you. The work depicts acts of self-harm, which he refuses to discuss. What do you do? How do you address confidentiality while fulfilling your duty to protect the client?

Cultural Sensitivity and Artistic Expression

- Your client creates art that holds symbolic, cultural meaning to them but is disturbing and conflict to your own cultural experience and values. What do you do? How do you navigate cultural interpretation without imposing biases?

Informed Consent and Therapeutic Boundaries

- Your client refuses to sign a consent form allowing you to use their artwork in a case study you hope to publish. During a later session, they provide verbal consent. Do you proceed with using the art?

Privacy/Confidentiality

- Your supervisor informs you that the sculpture one of your clients created during a session is too large to store in the filing room and should be kept out in your office (perhaps in the corner). How would you proceed?

The Takeaway

While art therapy shares common ethical foundations with other mental health professions, its unique integration of artistic processes introduces distinct ethical considerations. By adhering to principles of informed consent, trauma sensitivity, confidentiality, cultural competence, and ongoing professional development, therapists can foster a therapeutic environment that promotes healing and respects client autonomy.

Keystones

- Art therapists are guided by six core values of autonomy, justice, fidelity, creativity, nonmaleficence, and beneficence (AATA, 2013).
- Art therapists must only provide services they are trained for as evidenced by having a master's degree in art therapy reflecting core courses and supervised clinical hours (ATCB, 2024).
- Art therapists must be aware of cultural influences on clients' expressions, interpretations, and responses to art. They must also avoid appropriation and ensure an inclusive, respectful environment.

- Art therapists must explain the process, risks, benefits, expectations, and how the artwork will be used, stored, and disposed of to gain a client's informed consent.
- A unique challenge for art therapy practitioners is using artwork in clinical records. Due to space limitations, a photograph or detailed artwork description may be required rather than the piece itself.

ADDITIONAL RESOURCES

Di Maria, A. (Ed.). (2018). *Exploring ethical dilemmas in art therapy: 50 clinicians from 20 countries share their stories.* Routledge.

Hinz, L. D. (2011). Embracing excellence: A positive approach to ethical decision making. *Art Therapy: Journal of the American Art Therapy Association, 28*(4), 185–188.

Moon, B. L., & Nolan, E. G. (2020). *Ethical issues in art therapy* (4th ed.). Charles C. Thomas Publisher.

Talwar, S. (2017). Ethics, law, and cultural competence in art therapy. *Art Therapy, 34*(3), 102–105. https://doi.org/10.1080/07421656.2017.1358026

REFERENCES

American Art Therapy Association. (2011). *Art therapy multicultural/diversity competencies.* American Art Therapy Association. https://arttherapy.org/wp-content/uploads/2017/06/Multicultural-Competencies.pdf

American Art Therapy Association. (2013). *Ethical principles for art therapists.* American Art Therapy Association. https://arttherapy.org/ethics/

American Art Therapy Association. (2022). *Becoming an art therapist.* American Art Therapy Association. https://arttherapy.org/becoming-art-therapist/

American Counseling Association. (2014). *2014 ACA code of ethics.* American Counseling Association. https://www.counseling.org/docs/default-source/default-document-library/ethics/2014-aca-code-of-ethics.pdf

American Psychological Association. (2017). *Ethical principles of psychologists and code of conduct.* American Psychological Association. https://www.apa.org/ethics/code

American Psychological Association (2007). Record keeping guidelines. *The American Psychologist, 62*(9), 993–1004. https://doi.org/10.1037/0003-066X.62.9.993

Art Therapy Credentials Board. (2024). *Code governing Standards of Practice, Eligibility for and Regulation of Credentials and Disciplinary Procedures.* https://atcb.org/ethics-appeals-lp/code-of-ethics-conduct-and-disciplinary-procedures/

Atkins, M. (2007). Using digital photography to record clients' artwork. *International Journal of Art Therapy, 12*(2), 79–87. https://doi.org/10.1080/17454830701538410

Coles, A. (2018). The art of note writing: Art therapy and clinical notes (L'art de rédiger des notes: L'art-thérapie et les notes cliniques). *Canadian Art Therapy Association Journal, 31*(2), 101–104.

Hammond, L. C., & Gantt, L. (1998). Using art in counseling: Ethical considerations. *Journal of Counseling & Development, 76*(3), 271–276.

Hauck, J. M., Hughes, B. B., Ling, T. J., Jones, K., Eannone, C., Saltzman, S., Pacifico, A., Daquila, S. M., & Liu, T.-H. (2025). DRAWS: A documentation model for use in art therapy training and practice. *The Arts in Psychotherapy, 92*, 102246. https://www.sciencedirect.com/science/article/abs/pii/S019745562400131X#:~:text=DRAWS%20is%20a%20standardized%20note,unique%20to%20the%20creative%20process

Moon, B. (2000). *Ethical issues in art therapy.* Charles C. Thomas.

Morgan, K. (2023). Early-career art therapists reflecting client art in clinical notes: A thematic study. *International Journal of Art Therapy, 29*(3), 134–141. https://doi.org/10.1080/17454832.2023.2264372

Zawadi, N. K. (2024). Exploring ethical considerations in art therapy. *Research Invention Journal of Research in Education, 4*(1), 11–15. https://rijournals.com/wp-content/uploads/2024/11/RIJRE-41-2024-P3.pdf

Index

About the Author

Richard D. Parsons, PhD is Professor Emeritus in Counselor Education at West Chester University. He has over 45 years of university teaching experience and clinical practice.

Dr. Parsons has authored over 100 books, book chapters, and professional articles. His most recent books include *Positive Psychology: Science and Application of Psycho-Emotional Health and Well-Being, Brief Psychotherapy: Time-Limited and Effective Treatments*, and *Facilitating Growth Through Lifespan Development*, all published through Cognella Academic Publishing. Dr. Parsons also serves as the creator and editor of two book series, one a series of 24 books targeting counselor educators, Counseling and Professional Identity (Sage Publishing) and a 10-book series, the Cognella Series on Student Success (Cognella Academic Publishing).

www.ingramcontent.com/pod-product-compliance
Ingram Content Group UK Ltd.
Pitfield, Milton Keynes, MK11 3LW, UK
UKHW052009041026
15590UKWH00008B/2229

9 798823 384568